The New
Corporate Directors

The New Corporate Directors

Insights for Board Members and Executives

CHARLES A. ANDERSON

ROBERT N. ANTHONY

JOHN WILEY & SONS
New York · Chichester · Brisbane · Toronto · Singapore

This publication is designed to provide accurate and
authoritative information in regard to the subject
matter covered. It is sold with the understanding that
the publisher is not engaged in rendering legal, accounting,
or other professional service. If legal advice or other
expert assistance is required, the services of a competent
professional person should be sought. *From a Declaration
of Principles jointly adopted by a Committee of the
American Bar Association and a Committee of Publishers.*

Library of Congress Cataloging-in-Publication Data:

Anderson, Charles A., 1917–
    The new corporate directors.

    1. Directors of corporations.   I. Anthony, Robert
Newton, 1916–   . II. Title.

HD2745.A53   1986   658.4'22   86–5621
ISBN 0-471-84341-5

Printed in the United States of America

10 9 8 7 6 5 4 3 2 1

Preface

This book is about the job of being a corporate director. Those of us who are directors have important responsibilities to the shareowners and other constituencies of the corporations we serve. The vast majority of us want to fulfill our obligations effectively. This is not usually an easy assignment. From time to time we must make decisions crucial to our company's long-term future—even its survival. This book addresses our various responsibilities as directors, and it does so in the context of the real issues with which we must deal.

We do not have a list of eight rules for "excellence" or three "one-minute" prescriptions for the activities of an effective board. The CEO and the board members have differing abilities, backgrounds, and personalities. The problems confronting a board vary greatly from one organization to another. With such diversity, only a few principles, at most, are generally applicable.

What we do offer are some concepts and some ideas for directors to think about. They are not based on questionnaire surveys or on structured interviews. Rather, they grew out of experience, partly our own experience and partly the experience of friends who are CEOs, directors, or both. We respect their opinions.

v

As a device for organizing our views, we have prepared a number of short cases, each of which describes a particularly difficult issue with which directors must wrestle. These cases are based on real situations—they are not fictitious. They have, however, been disguised in order not to disclose either the companies or individuals involved. A number of people have been willing to read and react to these cases. Their reactions, together with our own, are reflected in the comments on each case. These cases and comments are an important part of this book.

These cases are in fact the reason that this book came to be written. Both of us have been on several corporate and nonprofit boards over a number of years, and from time to time we discussed with each other our board experiences. These discussions, it turned out, were helpful to us in clarifying concepts and principles involved in board membership, and it occurred to us that these might likewise be of interest to other board members. Over a period of several years, therefore, we prepared the cases in this book (with one exception). Some of them have been taught in programs at both the Harvard Business School and the Graduate School of Business at Stanford. Moreover, these cases and the text materials have been read by a number of our friends whom we regard as being unusually well qualified to comment on them.

We are especially grateful to Myles L. Mace and Kenneth R. Andrews of the Harvard Business School. Their years of both practical and academic experience with boards have provided them with a deep understanding of the issues that face directors, and we appreciate their generous help and encouragement. Eugene M. Zuckert and Carl A. Gerstacker, both experienced board members, likewise gave us many thoughtful and constructive suggestions. Many others have contributed to our knowledge of board matters and have influenced this book. We want especially to thank Ernest C. Arbuckle, Joseph Auerbach, Max Daetwyler, Gordon Donaldson, Neil E. Harlan, Robert K. Jaedicke, John Kircher, E. W. Littlefield, J. Sterling Livingston, Arjay Miller, Michael Morris, Shigeyoshi Takaoka, and E. Hornsby Wasson. We also thank Iva Podbilski for her help on all phases of this book. She has been secretary to one of us and friend of the other author for 26 years.

We have seen both effective and ineffective boards; practices that we thought were useful and others that were a waste of time; board members who were highly successful and those who didn't live up to their responsibilities. We are indebted to the many people—board chairmen and fellow board members—who collectively made possible the experiences that are the raw material used in writing this book.

For convenience, we use *he*, *him*, and *his* as neutral pronouns, referring equally to men and women.

CHARLES A. ANDERSON
ROBERT N. ANTHONY

Menlo Park, California
Waterville Valley, New Hampshire
May 1986

Acknowledgments

The Telemix Company case is condensed, with permission, from Chapters 3 and 4 of the doctoral dissertation of Natalie Tabb Taylor, *Management Succession Under Conditions of Crisis: The Role of the Board of Directors*, Graduate School of Business Administration, Harvard University (1978). Copyright © 1978 by Natalie Tabb Taylor.

The Tanner Company case is adapted with permission from Tanner Corporation, Harvard Business School case 176-036. Copyright © 1976 by the President and Fellows of Harvard College.

The article "Corporate Directors in Japan" by Charles A. Anderson originally appeared in *Harvard Business Review*, May/June 1984. Copyright © 1984 by the President and Fellows of Harvard College; all rights reserved. It is reproduced here by permission of the copyright owner.

C. A. A.
R. N. A.

Contents

1.	The Board and Corporate Governance	1
2.	The Director's Role	17
3.	The Role of the Chairman–CEO	47
4.	Dealing with Crises	63
5.	The Nominating Committee	87
6.	The Compensation Committee	111
7.	The Audit Committee	139
8.	The Finance Committee	169
9.	Nonprofit Organizations	193
10.	Trends	221
Appendix	Corporate Directors in Japan	229
Index		243

The New
Corporate Directors

1

The Board
and Corporate Governance

The functions that various people think actually *are performed* by a board of directors, and those functions that various people say *should* be performed, vary across a wide spectrum.

At one extreme, there are views such as the following:

The board of directors is an impotent ceremonial and legal fiction (Peter Drucker: management expert).

I proposed to charge the directors $250 a meeting for attending since they were learning more than we were (Robert Townsend, former chairman and CEO of Avis).

The board of directors has little choice but to follow meekly where the chief executive leads. Ninety-five percent are not fully doing what they are legally, morally, and ethically supposed to do (Harold Geneen, former chairman and CEO of ITT).

Although such descriptions may fit some boards, we do not believe them to be representative.

At the other end of the spectrum, statutes in some states say the board is responsible for *managing* the corporation. This theme is also expressed in several texts on management.

1

Moreover, it underlies the thinking of some who propose that corporations be federally chartered and that their boards function like government regulators.

A more constructive and realistic view than those quoted above is that of Harvard Professor Myles Mace, who believes, as we do, that the value of most boards lies someplace between these two extremes. Although widely known for his criticisms of the way many specific boards function, Mace's criticisms are accompanied by positive, practical suggestions for improvement.

Most boards, we believe, are made up of honest, competent people who sincerely want to carry out their duties effectively. To regard them as passive figureheads in the corporate structure is both unfair and inaccurate. Some boards may in fact be near-disasters, but others do a superb job. Most fall in the middle of this range. The purpose of this book is to help improve a system that works well, but which could be made to work better.

Eugene Zuckert, a long-time senior U.S. Government official and a wise and experienced corporate board member, has said that

> In the case of boards of directors, our expectations are so extravagant with such high potential for conflict that disappointment is inevitable. For example, we sometimes say we want a strong board that really runs the business. If pressed, we say we really don't want the board to run the business because that's a full-time job, and we don't expect the board to operate full time or anything like it. And besides, if we had a board that was too powerful, we probably could not get the strong CEO we need.

We believe it is the board's function to govern the corporation so that it serves the long-term interests of the shareowners and its other constituencies (employees, customers, suppliers, banks, community groups, labor unions, and other stakeholders). In carrying out this responsibility, the board members work most closely with the CEO, who is usually chairman of the board as well. An open, constructive working relationship between the outside directors and the CEO is an essential ingredient for an effective board. Nevertheless, this relationship inevitably involves a degree of tension. On one hand, the most important person in a corporation is its chief executive officer; the corporation's well-being depends above all else on how he manages it. On the other hand, the CEO is accountable to the board of directors, and the board must accept this responsibility without threatening the CEO's ability to manage. It is important to achieve a balance in this relationship.

A basic principle underlying the board's role is that anyone who exercises power needs to be accountable to someone else. A person who is not accountable, whose performance is immune to criticism and who cannot be removed from office, tends to become autocratic, arbitrary, and insensitive to the views of others. Such an individual is obviously unsuitable for the management of a complex organization. The board, by overseeing the CEO's performance, helps to keep things running smoothly. This should not imply an atmosphere of antagonism or distrust. The board and the CEO should cooperate, not compete. In ideal circumstances, the attitude of the board toward the CEO and of the CEO toward the board is one of mutual respect and support.

THE BOARD'S RESPONSIBILITIES

In doing its job, the board should accept certain responsibilities. These are listed briefly below. (In later chapters, we shall expand on them.) It should:

1. Actively support the CEO and his policies, both within the organization and to outside parties, as long as his performance is judged to be generally satisfactory.
2. Replace the CEO promptly if it concludes that his performance is, and will continue to be, unsatisfactory.
3. Ensure, to the extent feasible, that the CEO has identified his successor and is grooming him for the job.
4. Participate actively in decisions to elect or reelect directors.

5. Decide on policies relating to compensation of senior management, including bonuses, incentives, and perquisites. Determine the compensation of the CEO. Review recommendations of the CEO and ratify compensation of other executives.

6. Discuss proposed major changes in the company's strategy and direction, major financing proposals, and other crucial issues, usually as proposed by the CEO. Reach its own decision on these matters (as contrasted with the ratification of other decisions, as described in the next paragraph).

7. Require that the CEO explain the rationale behind operating budgets, major capital expenditures, acquisitions, divestments, dividends, personnel matters (including matters relating to strikes) and similar important plans. Accept these proposals if they are consistent with the company's strategy and if the explanation is reasonable. Otherwise, require additional information.

8. Formulate major policies regarding ethical or public responsibility matters and convey to the organization the fact that the board expects adherence to these policies. Assure that violations of these policies are not tolerated.

9. Analyze reports on the company's performance, raise questions to highlight areas of possible concern, and suggest possible actions to improve performance, but always with the understanding that the CEO, not the board, is responsible for performance.

10. Assure that financial information furnished to shareowners and other outside parties fairly presents the financial performance and status of the company. Assure that internal controls are satisfactory.

THE BOARD'S ACTIVITIES

In order to fulfill the above responsibilities, the board should have the following characteristics:

1. It should consist, ideally, of ten to eighteen members. (A larger board can handle its responsibilities if it delegates many of them to committees, and if there is an understanding that committee recommendations will be accepted with little debate.)

2. Most of the members should be outsiders: that is, they should not be company executives. In a chapter on the nominating committee, we discuss the selection of outside directors in some detail. In addition to the CEO, the insiders, or company executives, often include candidates to succeed the CEO. They are on the board so that the members can get to know them and appraise their qualifications. (Other employees are invited to board meetings as necessary.)

3. The board should meet regularly between six and eleven times a year (with special meetings as needed). Most meetings last less than a day, but informal discussions and homework make the time required somewhat more than a day, considerably more if the member lives at a distance. Annually or biannually, there may be a meeting to review strategy, and it may last for a day or more.

4. In advance of the meeting, board members should be furnished with material on current performance and on issues to be discussed at the meeting.

5. Before, and sometimes after, the formal meeting, there should be opportunities for informal interchanges between board members and between the board and members of senior management.

6. The chairman should be a full-time company employee, usually the CEO. The chairman has other duties unrelated to his function as chairman. (In a few instances, an outsider is chairman.)

7. Much of the board's work should be done through committees. These include at least a compensation committee and an audit committee. There may be other committees, including (but not limited to) nominating, finance, and

public policy committees. The necessary staff work for the committees is done by company employees.

THE BOARD PROCESS

A good board is characterized by a membership of able, independent people with differing backgrounds, abilities, and temperaments, who are willing to express—and to listen respectfully to—varying viewpoints. Such a board, with good leadership, will engage in healthy and sometimes vigorous discussion on corporate issues and problems. Out of such debate, decisions are reached which the board can support. A wide variety of backgrounds and experience can in itself make a board a rich and valuable resource for the company. (It also makes an interesting experience for the board members themselves.)

ORGANIZATION OF THE BOARD

In the next three chapters we will expand on the decision-making process of the board as a whole. Following these, we will discuss more specific board functions in chapters dealing with the nominating committee, the compensation committee, the audit committee, and the finance committee. While all boards may not appoint these specific committees, those areas of responsibility seem the most essential to discuss. Other committees can, of course, be appointed but do not usually form the backbone of the board's organization.

For instance, an *executive committee* can be empowered to act between board meetings. In a few companies, this committee makes the principal decisions, and the full board merely ratifies them. More commonly, though, the executive committee exists primarily to handle emergencies and is otherwise inactive.

Some boards also appoint a *public policy* or *public responsibility* committee. This group might:

- Ensure that the company has an adequate antidiscrimination policy and complies with it in letter and spirit.
- Find out whether the company has satisfactory relations with the employees' communities.
- Consider alleged deficiencies in relations with customers, product quality and safety, pollution, occupational safety and health, and employee relations, ensuring that corrective action is taken if the allegations are warranted.
- Receive reports on actual or pending litigation or government complaints, particularly on product liability or environmental quality litigation, and satisfy itself that management is responding properly to the threats.
- Recommend what stance, if any, the company should take with respect to proposed legislation.

An important rationale for creating such a committee is that a small group can deal with sensitive matters that would be awkward if discussed in a large board meeting.

CONCLUSION

Boards of directors play an important—often vital—role in the life of a corporation, and it is important that they function effectively. While recognizing that boards are imperfect, we believe that most board members are serious about their obligations and seek to do a responsible job. By examining how other boards do their work, as in the following case study, we believe that directors can find ways to improve their own effectiveness.

CASE
Cleary Company—The Solitary "No" Vote

On March 28, 1980, Marvin Hatfield cast his first "No" vote during the 13 years he had been director of Cleary Company. In retrospect, he wondered whether he should have done this.

Cleary Company was a century-old company that manufactured and sold power tools and other hardware and building supply items. Its tools were sold under several brand names to consumers. Some product lines, such as logging equipment, were developed specifically for industrial customers. The company had had its ups and downs, but in the 1970s, under the leadership of James Fallon, its sales and profits grew rapidly. In 1978 net income was $22 million on sales volume of $410 million.

In January 1979 its board consisted of James Fallon, chairman and CEO; Walter Evans, president and chief operating officer; Charles Lottman, financial vice president; Francis Sterling, senior vice president; four outside directors experienced in the industry; the CEOs of two large companies in other industries; a senior vice president of Cleary's lead bank, and Marvin Hatfield, senior partner in a management consulting firm.

In July 1979, Fallon died suddenly. Walter Evans, age 50, was being groomed as the next CEO, and in a meeting held the day of the funeral he was elected CEO. The election was enthusiastic, even though board members thought that further experience would have been desirable. Two months after becoming CEO, Evans described some of his plans at a board meeting. He stressed the desirability of making certain types of acquisitions. Cleary Company had made only minor acquisitions since 1965.

Meadville Hardware Company. Early in October 1979, Evans sent board members information about the proposed acquisition of Meadville Hardware Company. He described the proposal at the October 26 board meeting. A price had not been negotiated. The board approved the acquisition in principle at that time. Shortly before the January 1980 Board meeting, the directors were sent a two-page summary of the proposed terms, together with an estimate that the acquisition would earn a return of 16 percent on its investment.

Hatfield did not understand how the 16 percent ROI had been calculated. He held several phone conversations with Charles

Lottman, financial vice president, and Edmund Smale (who analyzed proposed acquisitions) to find out the procedure followed and assumptions made. The proposed terms involved $23 million cash at the time of closing, consulting arrangements with the current management, and a payout to be made five years later, with the amount depending on the acquisition's profitability during the five years. Although he was not completely satisfied with Smale's analysis, Hatfield recognized that calculating an ROI for such a complicated proposal was inherently uncertain, and he decided to support the proposed acquisition.

In the January 1980 board meeting, Hatfield stated that he hoped that a more thorough explanation of the calculations would be furnished in connection with any future acquisition. No other director questioned either the general desirability of acquiring the company, the specifics of the terms, or the ROI calculation, and no one expressed dissatisfaction with the information furnished the board.

The minutes of the January 1980 Board meeting contained the following:

Mr. Hatfield indicated concern regarding the return on investment, particularly questioning the limited upside opportunity during the five-year earn-out period. After complete discussion, upon motion duly made and seconded, the Directors unanimously approved the acquisition of Meadville Hardware Company, in accordance with the proposal as presented to the meeting.

Shortly thereafter the principal shareholder of Meadville Hardware Company changed his mind about selling his company, so this deal was not consummated.

Townes Corporation Acquisition. At the January 1980 meeting, Evans also reported that the acquisition of Townes Corporation was being seriously explored and that the price would be in the neighborhood of $24 million. Shortly thereafter the directors were sent about 50 pages of historical information about

Townes Corporation, including financial statements for each of its divisions, a description of each plant and other real estate, a description of each product line and its estimated market share, the marketing organization, its research/development program, and important customers. After receiving this information, Hatfield wrote Evans reminding him of the request for a thorough analysis of the acquisition price and spelling out his ideas on how such an analysis should be made. Evans replied in a letter, stating that "we will present data to the board in great depth, although we may not be able to fill the exact requests of all directors because this could be unduly cumbersome."

On March 10, 1980, the directors were sent a one-page summary of the proposed purchase terms: a payment of $24 million cash in exchange for Townes Corporation stock and some minor provisions, such as continuing the Townes profit-sharing plan. The directors were also sent a sheet headed "projected financial results," which contained three lines of numbers with projections for each of the five years 1980–1984: (1) sales, which was a projection of 10 percent growth each year, (2) pretax income, which was based on a margin of 10 percent in 1980, increasing to 12 percent in 1984, and (3) addition to EPS, derived from the profit estimate. The sheet also reported that the return on investment would be 24.2 percent.

Hatfield telephoned Lottman, the financial vice president, requesting additional information, and in Lottman's absence talked with Edmund Smale, who was responsible for the detailed analysis. During the lengthy conversation, Hatfield pointed out that the calculation of ROI contained a significant error and moreover no allowance had been made for the investment in additional working capital that would be required by the sales increase.

The next day Smale telephoned Hatfield and said that he and Lottman agreed that the ROI was incorrectly calculated and that additional working capital would be required. However, these two changes were partially offset by an increase in the price at which it was assumed that Townes could be sold for in 1985, and the net effect was to revise the ROI to 20 percent. Hatfield thought that the estimates were unduly optimistic; he made a more conservative calculation that led to an ROI of 15 percent. Lottman disagreed with Hatfield's assumptions.

Although there were several more phone conversations, there was no change in the position of either Hatfield or Lottman. Hatfield finally said that although he did not question the excellence of Townes Corporation, he would not vote in favor of paying $24 million for it.

At the board meeting on March 28, 1980, the proposed acquisition was submitted for approval. During this meeting, Hatfield announced that he could not support the proposal, giving his reasons. No other director supported him, and no one asked for a further explanation. One outside director suggested that Hatfield should reconsider his position in the interest of unanimity; but Evans, the CEO, responded that he felt that each director should vote as his judgment dictated. The acquisition was approved with one negative vote.

The next meeting of the board was held on April 25. Just prior to that meeting, Evans took Hatfield aside and said that a problem had arisen. The law of the state in which Townes was incorporated permitted directors to approve a merger only if the directors of both corporations were unanimously in favor of the merger. If there was no unanimity, the shareholders of the acquired corporation would have to vote on the proposal. Calling a shareholder meeting would require a month or more, and this delay could upset the whole deal. Hatfield said that in these circumstances he would change his vote and support the proposal, and he did this during the April 25 meeting.

After the April 25 meeting, Hatfield questioned in his own mind whether he had acted correctly. Should he be a maverick on a proposition favored by management and all his colleagues? On the other hand, if he voted for something he thought was wrong, was he being only a rubber stamp, and if so, what function did he perform as a director? But was his position genuine, or did it reflect primarily his pique about the skimpy set of numbers, which indicated a disregard of his request for a thorough analysis? Even if the latter, how could he persuade management to furnish the information he believed the directors needed if this, the second incident involving inadequate analysis, was permitted to pass without challenge? Was his posture antagonizing his colleagues and thus lessening his effectiveness on other matters?

Our Comment on Cleary Company

Nearly every conscientious board member at one time or another has faced the dilemma that Marvin Hatfield did. We believe he did the right thing in casting the solitary "no" vote on March 22, 1980. In the long run his action might well have had a salutary effect. Moreover, while we respect his sensitivity concerning the attitude of his fellow directors, no one should be offended or take exception when a director votes as his conscience dictates.

The case makes it clear that Hatfield was a director who did his homework. In the 1979 proposed acquisition of Meadville Hardware (which did not go through), he went on record as questioning the basis for determining the projected ROI. He also expressed the hope that management would furnish the board with a more complete explanation of how it had arrived at the projected rate of return. Hatfield reminded Evans of his request after receiving 50 pages of information about Townes, which included no analysis of the return on investment. He even outlined his ideas of how this analysis might be made. The information furnished was sparse, and Hatfield had every right to request more information, as well as to be slightly miffed at not having had his request taken more seriously.

It seems evident that Hatfield was experienced—undoubtedly from his consulting practice—in the various ways of computing anticipated returns on acquisitions. Indeed, in view of the fact that following a discussion with management the projected ROI was reduced from 24.2 percent to 20 percent, one can conclude that Hatfield was probably more knowledgeable in this area than management. It is true that projections of this type involve a good deal of subjective judgment. They are inherently imprecise. However, the flaws that Hatfield discovered were material, and they raised a question as to the credibility of the financial staff's numbers. A board should expect—indeed require—that a projection on which such an important decision is to be based will be made according to high professional standards. This was Hatfield's role as a director, and this is what he was trying to do.

It is noteworthy—and to his credit—that Evans, the CEO, made no effort to influence Hatfield to change his negative vote, even though one of the outside directors suggested this. It seems likely, or at least possible, that when the next acquisition appears on the horizon Evans will see to it that the financial data related to the transaction are reviewed with Hatfield in advance of presentation to the full board. In fact, it might be smart, while the incident is still fresh, for Hatfield to approach Evans and thank him for his understanding, as reflected by his willingness to let Hatfield's no vote stand at the March 28 meeting. He could say that he in no way meant the vote as lack of support for Evans or his management. He could add that in future instances he would be willing, to help avoid undue embarrassment, to review and comment on financial data and projections in advance of board meetings.

A comment concerning unanimity of board action is appropriate. In many boards, and for some CEOs, there seems to be an "ethic" that says: "Unless you vote with the management you are committing a disloyal act and are thereby being divisive." This is not a constructive attitude. A good board member should be expected to exercise his independent judgment. If this means that a board member occasionally dissents from a management recommendation, so be it. It is this give and take among board members—the flexibility, patience, and constructive approach to group discussion—that makes for good decisions.

Of course, if a board member finds himself repeatedly in disagreement with management and the rest of the board, there is probably a deep-seated problem. However, in Hatfield's case, one disagreement in 13 years clearly cannot be regarded as lack of support for management or as evidence of dissension within the board.

A further observation concerns the board's role in setting standards for management. If a board member believes that a piece of work—be it an earnings projection, a market research analysis, or a product design—is sloppily or superficially done, he should bring it to management's attention and make it clear that the work is not satisfactory. This should not be a confrontational act accompanied by fire and invectives. It should be done quietly and courteously. Nevertheless, the point should be made. Otherwise the board member is failing to set a standard with which he is comfortable. We believe that Hatfield was trying to set better standards for the company's financial analysis of proposed acquisitions. This was entirely proper.

There is, however, one cautionary comment that relates to Hatfield's interactions with the Cleary Company's financial staff. In his earlier dealings with Lottman and Smale, Hatfield could have alienated them by his persistent questioning of their work. In the Townes acquisition they may have dug in their heels and decided that they were not going to allow Hatfield to push them around—or to make them appear to be professionally deficient in the eyes of their boss, Evans. As it turned out, Lottman must have been chagrined at having to reduce his projected ROI. To have reduced it further would have been tantamount to admitting his incompetence. However, by dealing directly with Lottman and Smale, Hatfield was on dangerous ground. He could be accused of meddling with Evan's organization. If he persists in going around Evans (if indeed that was the case) and trying to tell the financial staff how to do its work, Evans would have to take a stand. The CEO cannot and should not allow a board member to direct the activities of his executive staff.

It is conceivable that Hatfield concluded, on the basis of his prior interactions with the organization, that the CEO relied on his financial vice president to handle problems in this area, and that the CEO preferred that his own time not be taken up with them. If, but only if, this conclusion was correct, Hatfield's course of action was understandable. In general, however, a director must be careful not to interfere with the CEO's organization.

2

The Director's Role

An outsider who reads the minutes of board meetings might reasonably conclude that a director's duties are largely ceremonial. If a board is ineffective, this impression would be correct. An effective board, however, performs important functions that are not adequately described in the minutes. We discuss the board's most important functions in this chapter. The first sections focus on these functions in a publicly owned company, and a later section describes the somewhat different functions in a private company.

OUTWARD APPEARANCES

From the minutes, one would get the following impression of the typical board meeting:

The meeting lasts for two or three hours. In the first hour or so, the CEO and other senior officers summarize the company's recent performance and the outlook for its immediate future. Much of what is said about performance is already known to the directors from information sent to them prior to the meeting. They ask a few questions, and they volunteer opinions about what is likely to happen to the economy and to the company's industry.

The CEO answers their questions or says that the answers will be furnished later. The CEO thanks them for their insights.

Next, a number of proposed actions are submitted for board approval. Many of these recommendations come to the full board from committees that have discussed the topics in meetings held prior to the board meeting. Questions may be raised about these recommendations, but these are usually requests for clarification. The full board approves them, often with little or no debate on the substance.

Next, the board covers a number of routine items, each of which is faithfully listed on the agenda. These may be requests for approval of capital projects, approval of signature authority for various banking connections, approval of exceptions to pension plans, approval of certain types of contracts, and so on. Except for large capital projects, these items are usually referred to as *boilerplate*. In most cases, they come to the board because state law, the corporate bylaws, or written policy requires board action. They are approved with little discussion, sometimes en bloc, despite the fact that the minutes may state for each of them: after a full discussion, a motion to adopt the recommendation was duly made and seconded, and the motion was approved.

Finally, a division manager assisted by senior associates may make a presentation, which includes numerous graphs and tables. He describes the activities and plans for the division, usually in glowing terms.

The meeting then adjourns for lunch, dinner, or a social occasion.

THE REAL AGENDA

Many of the events described above do not appear to be, and in fact are not, important to the well being of the company; they are indeed boilerplate. Other issues warrant, and receive, thoughtful discussion by the board; approval of major capital projects is an example. In addition to thinking about these matters, the effective director is engaged in other activities that, although nowhere stated in the minutes, are of crucial importance. Among these are:

1. Watching for trouble.
2. Preparing for a crisis.
3. Appraising the CEO.
4. Forming a judgment about the next CEO.
5. Setting standards of performance.
6. Influencing strategy.

Watching for Trouble

Prior to each regular board meeting, directors normally receive a packet of material that includes current financial information. They need to study this information carefully, looking specifically for possible weak spots. At the board meeting the CEO or another senior officer discusses the company's current situation and his own assessment of the future. Each director should be prepared to raise questions, based on his homework and on the additional information provided at the meeting. If time permits, the director should raise some of these questions by telephone prior to the meeting. If the answers are satisfactory, this saves time at the meeting, and avoids the embarrassing possibility of asking a question whose answer is obvious.

The financial information probably includes condensed income statements for each division, or for groups of divisions if the company has a large number of divisions; key balance sheet items, such as inventory and receivable amounts; and corporate expenses. There are three formats for presenting financial information

1. Comparison of management's current estimate of performance for the whole year with budgeted performance for the year: How do we now estimate that the company is going

to perform for the whole year? This is the most important type of information. However, it is also the most sensitive, and many companies do not circulate it prior to the meeting.

2. Comparison of actual performance for the current period and for the year to date with budgeted performance for these periods. Since the actual numbers are firm, they provide a more objective basis for analysis than the current estimate referred to above.

3. Comparison of actual performance with performance for the same periods last year. This comparison reflects the preference of some directors for such an analysis. A carefully prepared budget incorporates changes in the business and the economy that have occurred since the prior year. Such a budget is therefore a more meaningful basis for comparison than last year's numbers. If, however, the budgeted amounts, particularly the estimate of revenue, are highly uncertain, the numbers for last year provide a firmer foundation for a comparison.

Since few companies can predict sales with a high degree of accuracy, differences between budgeted and actual amounts are to be expected. The hope is that poorer-than-budgeted performance in some divisions will be offset by better performance in others, or that shortfalls in some periods will be balanced by excellent performance in other periods. Thus, unfavorable revenue or profit variances, especially if they are transitory, are not by themselves cause for alarm. Ordinarily, the CEO will have an adequate explanation for them. Expenses usually can be budgeted with greater confidence than revenues, so a significant difference between actual and budgeted expenses automatically suggests that a question be raised.

Preparing for a Crisis

Specific crisis situations are discussed in Chapter 4. They arise rarely—so rarely that a board member may serve for decades without facing one. A crisis occurs unexpectedly, and when one does surface, the continued existence of the company may depend on the way the board deals with it. These situations usually cannot be resolved solely on the basis of a management recommendation. This is obviously the case if replacement of the CEO is one possible course of action. In other crisis situations, such as an unfriendly tender offer, the interests of the CEO may be different from those of the company.

Effective directors do as much as they can to prepare themselves to deal with a crisis. They learn about the company—its competitive strengths and weaknesses, the strengths and weaknesses of specific competitors, and the characteristics of its industry. They observe members of senior management to gauge the weight that should be given to their opinions, how strong their loyalty is, and how compatible they are with one another. They observe their colleagues on the board for the same purpose and also to assess who probably can be counted on to support, and who are likely to oppose, a course of action that they may decide to advocate.

Appraising the CEO

The chief executive officer is responsible for the company's performance. If performance is below expectations, there are two possible explanations: (1) The CEO is to blame, or (2) extraneous influences are responsible. In most cases, both factors are involved, and the directors have the extraordinarily difficult job of judging their relative importance. If they conclude that the CEO has made an incorrect decision, they may suggest a different course of action. More likely, however, they say nothing and mentally file the incident for future reference in evaluating the CEO. The Business Roundtable, a group of CEOs of leading companies, succinctly described the directors' role vis-a-vis the CEO as "challenging, yet supportive and positive."

Thus, the primary function of the review of operations that occupies much time at a board meeting is not to provide the director with a basis of critiquing performance or for making suggestions for improvement. Rather, from the director's viewpoint, its primary purpose is to appraise the CEO (and other senior managers who participate in the review). Directors usually cannot make constructive suggestions on the details of current operations. Occasionally, they may call attention to a matter that should be looked into. Primarily, however, they listen carefully to what the CEO says, and do their best to judge whether things are going satisfactorily and, if not, where the responsibility lies.

The directors want the CEO to be frank and to give an accurate analysis of the company's status and prospects; concealing bad news is one of the worst sins a CEO can commit. Nevertheless, human nature is such that directors cannot expect the CEO to be completely objective. Incipient problems may go away, and making them known, even in the relative privacy of the boardroom, may cause unnecessary alarm. An effective director is therefore on the alert for indications of significant problems that may lie ahead. In many of the well publicized bankruptcies of public companies, the directors were significantly responsible; they did not identify or act on the problem soon enough.

Louis B. Cabot, chairman of the board of Cabot Corporation, had a frustrating experience with the ill-fated Penn Central corporation, one of the largest bankruptcies that had occurred up to that time. He joined the Penn Central board about a year before the company went under. From the outset, he was disturbed by management's unwillingness to furnish the information about performance that he felt he needed. A few months after joining the board he wrote the CEO a letter that contains a succinct description of the director's role:

> I believe directors should not be the managers of a business, but they should ensure the excellence of its management by appraising that management's performance. To do this, they have to measure that performance against agreed-upon yardsticks.

Unfortunately, some directors comment on the review of operations primarily for the purpose of demonstrating to their colleagues that they have read all the preliminary material, that they are genuinely interested in what is going on, or that they are experts in the topics being discussed. Comments made for these reasons are not ordinarily a good use of time.

The Next CEO

The board selects the CEO, and this is usually the most important decision a board makes. As soon as one CEO has been elected, the effective director starts thinking about that CEO's successor. Although directors usually must rely on the CEO to identify individuals within the company who are potential candidates, each director forms a personal opinion about the relative merits of each individual so identified. These judgments may develop over a period of years, and they are subject to change as new evidence comes to light. When the time comes to act—either at the CEO's normal retirement, or earlier if the unexpected happens—the directors should be confidently prepared to select a successor.

An effective board has a regular procedure for reviewing succession plans. Although this process culminates in discussing who should succeed the CEO, it is usually not limited to that one position. All key executives are reviewed. How are they progressing? What is their potential? Are their successors identified? In Carborundum Company for example, Bill Wendel, the chairman, annually convened an informal meeting of the outside directors, solely to discuss succession. Directors referred to it as the "truck meeting" because Bill always started with the question. Suppose I am run over by a truck tomorrow; what will you do? At Carborundum, two and sometimes three, persons were identified as potential CEOs. As time went on, individuals were added to, or eliminated from, the list, and their relative ranking changed. With this type of process, the directors can make an intelligent choice whenever the need arises. (Unfortunately, Carborundum was acquired by another company, and that company was in turn acquired; the Carborundum board ceased to exist, and its carefully laid plans came to naught. This is the way the cookie sometimes crumbles.)

For various reasons, some sound and some not so sound, the directors may end up selecting an outsider as the next CEO. In many cases, this is an indication that the directors themselves have not done an adequate job of arranging for succession.

Setting Standards

Partly through written policy statements, but primarily through their personal attitudes, effective directors communicate to management the standards that they believe should govern the organization's actions. There are two general types of standards, which might be labelled *economic standards* and *ethical standards*, although neither term is precisely correct.

With respect to economic standards, the directors communicate the overall goals that they believe the company can and should attain: the relative importance of sales growth, earnings per share, and return on investment, and the specific numbers that they believe to be attainable. They indicate the relative importance to short-run versus long-run performance. (For example, if they want the focus to be on the long run, they do not criticize a relatively poor earnings record in the current quarter.) They express concern if the debt/equity ratio appears to be getting out of line, in either direction. For the specifics, they generally rely on management's recommendations, but the enthusiasm, or lack of enthusiasm, with which they support a given recommendation conveys important information to management.

Ethical standards are nebulous. The written policy statements are always impeccably virtuous, but the actual expectations of the directors are indicated by the way they react to specific ethical problems. It is easy to rely on counsel's answer to the question: Must we report this unpleasant development to the SEC? The answer depends on the legal interpretation of the regulations. It is much more difficult for the directors to agree, and to convey to management, that a certain course of action, although perhaps within the letter of the law, should not be tolerated. For example, the stated hiring, promotion, or other personnel practices may explicitly forbid race, gender, or other discrimination, but the directors may observe with their own eyes that inbalances probably exist. Currently, directors of many companies must wrestle with the policy toward operations in South Africa: Although it is perfectly legal to be there, does a company's presence do more harm than good?

Influencing Strategy

The board rarely has the knowledge necessary for initiating a strategy or for choosing among alternative strategies. It must rely on management to take the initiative, make the necessary analyses, and bring its recommendations to the board. What the board can and should do is described by Kenneth Andrews in his book, *The Concept of Corporate Strategy*. Andrew writes, as a summary:

A responsible and effective board should require of its management a unique and durable corporate strategy, review it periodically for its validity, use it as the reference point for all other board decisions, and share with management the risks associated with its adoption.

The board exercises its responsibility through (1) decisions made at regular board meetings, and (2) meetings that focus specifically on the company's strategies.

STRATEGY DECISIONS AT NORMAL BOARD MEETINGS. Certain matters that come to the board for action have a significant influence on the future of the company. The strategic decisions made today will require that money be spent tomorrow, and the expectation is that this will generate more money in the future. Acquisitions and divestitures are obvious examples of strategic proposals that require the board's careful consideration. The long-term impact of capital expenditures is less obvious, and directors are sometimes inclined to treat these as routine agenda items, not worthy of much thought or discussion. Directors may assume that management has thoroughly analyzed the benefits and costs of the proposed capital expenditure and that this analysis can be relied on. Such an assumption gives more credit to the validity of analytical techniques than is warranted.

There are indeed good techniques for estimating the net present value of certain types of proposed capital expenditures, and directors should insist that these be used. They apply, however, to only a minority of proposals because, although the cost of many capital projects can be estimated with reasonable accuracy, the benefits—in terms of increased sales volume, productivity, product quality, or other factors—are usually highly uncertain. For important proposals, therefore, directors should satisfy themselves that management's assumptions are reasonable, reflect all available information, and are evaluated using the best techniques possible.

Directors should consider these proposals in the context of the broad strategies that have previously been adopted. Is the proposal consistent with these strategies, or does it imply some new direction? In the latter, have the implications on the company's strategy been carefully considered?

STRATEGY MEETINGS. The company should have a set of objectives, that is, the businesses it wants to be in, and general strategies that provide guidance as to how it will operate in these businesses, (e.g., high quality, high margins, and lower market share versus lower margins and mass marketing). It is a good idea to put these guidelines into writing. Strategies are not immutable; they are subject to change as conditions warrant. However, changing them requires a more rigorous analysis than does adhering to them.

While it is unrealistic to expect directors to formulate strategies, they should satisfy themselves that management has a sound

process for developing them. The strategy is probably acceptable
if

- It is based on careful analysis by people who are in the best position to evaluate it, rather than on an inspiration accepted without study;
- The reasoning seems sensible;
- The director is not aware of significant information that has been omitted from the analysis; and
- The results expected from the strategy are clearly set forth so that actual accomplishment can be compared with them.

As a basis for considering the strategic planning process, many companies arrange a meeting at which directors, together with senior managers, spend one, two, or three days discussing where the company should be headed. In order to minimize distractions and to provide an opportunity for informal discussion and reflection, these meetings are often held at a retreat, distant from the corporate offices. Because of the time required, these strategy meetings are usually held not more than once every two years.

The primary purpose of a strategy meeting is to explain the strategies and the foundations on which they are based. The explanations themselves provide useful information to the directors. The quality of the rationale for the strategies is an indication of the competence of senior management and of the managers of the divisions concerned. Thus, the strategies provide additional insight about the CEO's abilities, and about the abilities of participants who may be candidates for CEO. The social side of the retreat provides additional opportunities for forming impressions about members of management and colleagues on the board.

Some members of management overestimate the director's ability to absorb detail. In these circumstances, presentations at meetings may be numbing, leaving the directors more confused than educated.

CHARACTERISTICS OF EFFECTIVE MEETINGS

Following are suggestions for arranging both regular meetings
and retreats so as to improve the chances of accomplishing what
the meetings are supposed to accomplish.

Number of Meetings

The number of meetings held annually depends primarily on how
long a period is likely to elapse before serious trouble surfaces.
Presumably, the minimum is four meetings per year, because the
directors must approve the quarterly dividend declaration (although such approval could be given at a telephone meeting).
However, four meetings is ordinarily enough only in a company
that operates in a reasonably stable environment. Some boards
find that eight meetings, two per quarter, are adequate; others
prefer 11, one a month except during August.

Homework

Prior to each meeting, effective directors do their homework.
They must rely on whatever information the CEO chooses to send
them. Since the CEO wants to accommodate their need for information to the extent practical, directors should make their
needs known. For example, if in the regular meeting the CEO
spends time explaining what part of an unfavorable revenue var-
iance is attributable to sales volume and what part to off-price
sales, a director may point out that these variances can easily be
calculated and stated in the regular financial report, and thus
save time at the meeting.

Such suggestions for improvement are best initiated in informal discussions, either directly with the CEO or with whoever
is responsible for compiling the information. If informal suggestions are disregarded, it is then appropriate to bring the matter
up during the board meeting.

A study of the information provided prior to a board meeting may suggest questions to a director. Many of these can be raised and answered by telephone or by informal conversation before the meeting. This saves meeting time and reduces the possibility that the director will ask a stupid question in the meeting. For each question he has, the director must decide whether it should be asked directly of the CEO or raised with some other executive. On the one hand, the director does not want to give the impression of bypassing the CEO, but on the other hand he does not want to use the CEO's time unnecessarily. By means of trials (and hopefully not too many errors), each director learns the appropriate course of action.

Although a preliminary agenda is often sent to directors before a meeting, it does not list all the items that will be taken up. Some of them are so sensitive that they should not be described ahead of time. (This contrasts with the annual meeting of shareowners where no action can be taken on an item that was not previously described in the proxy statement.)

Contrary to the usual advice, we do not believe that directors must spend a lot of time preparing for every board meeting. If the current situation is satisfactory and if there are no important issues requiring background information, why should anyone feel obligated to spend a prescribed number of hours on homework?

The Board Meeting

At his first meeting, the director is well advised to say very little. He has a lot to learn, and he must recognize that the time available for discussion at a board meeting is limited. He therefore keeps quiet unless he has something constructive to say. After the introductory meeting, some participation in most meetings is desirable in order to establish a presence.

The director may come to a meeting with questions suggested by the homework that have not been answered by informal conversations prior to the meeting. If the CEO answers these questions in the course of his summary, the director discards them. If not, the most important one or two of them can be asked. One caution: If a question has been answered previously, asking it again does the director's reputation no good. For example, if administrative expenses for the year to date exceed budget, the explanation may have been given at an earlier meeting, and the alert director remembers this fact.

If a director can supplement the CEO's presentation with comments based on his special knowledge of technical developments, the market, the economy, or the financial situation, he should feel free to do so, always with recognition of the limitations of available time.

In many meetings there is no genuine debate, nor is there a need for debate. In some meetings there is an informed difference of opinion on an important issue, and in these circumstances the issue should be thrashed out. Such a debate exposes a variety of viewpoints, often reveals points that have not yet been considered, and is likely to lead either to an informed acceptance of the proposal or to a better solution. Alternatively, the discussion may suggest the need for further information, and action may be deferred to a later meeting.

To the extent feasible, the CEO should be supported. When a majority is reluctant to accept the CEO's recommendation, a graceful solution may be to refer the matter back for further study. In this way the interval before the next meeting can be used for informal discussions.

The CEO may lay the foundation for discussion of an important matter that is not on the formal agenda but will be brought to the board at a future meeting: an acquisition, a divestiture, introduction of a new product line, construction of a major plant, closing of a plant, or a reorganization. The CEO sketches the proposed course of action in general terms and tries to assess the directors' attitude toward it from their questions and comments. Based on his sense of what is needed, he develops additional information that is sent to board members later on. This discussion helps the CEO and motivates the directors to start thinking about the issue.

Above all else, the director should be alert to nuances that help him make judgments about the topics listed in the preceding section: Is the company headed for trouble? If so, is the CEO responsible? Is the CEO being completely frank? What are the predilections of his fellow directors? Who should be the next CEO?

Informal Activities

What goes on outside the board room is fully as important as what goes on inside. Social activities provide the director with a means of assessing the abilities and points of view of fellow directors and members of management, of picking up useful gossip about what is going on in the company, and of selling his own point of view. It also provides an environment for forming and strengthening friendships, which is one of the features that makes a directorship attractive. The wise CEO will provide for these opportunities in the form of luncheons or dinners, either before or after meetings. Inviting spouses to some of these occasions can add to the atmosphere.

We do not regard plant visits as being particularly useful in aiding the director's understanding of the technical aspects of production, or in providing expert advice. Even a board member with extensive production experience is unlikely to come up with important suggestions on the basis of the necessarily brief and superficial exposure. Nevertheless, plant visits do have other important functions. They give the directors a feel for the company's business, its facilities and its people; they show local management and employees that directors are interested in their activities. Perhaps most importantly, plant visits usually require that the directors be together for at least a whole day, outside of the normal routine—in the case of a foreign visit, for perhaps the better part of a week. This gives the directors an opportunity to know one another better and to know senior management better.

Meetings with groups of customers, attendance at conventions, and other activities related to marketing can be similarly productive.

The Annual Meeting

The functions of directors at the annual shareowners meeting is to be present, to make and second the motions called for in the agenda, to support management if called upon to do so, and otherwise to keep quiet.

BOARDS OF PRIVATE COMPANIES

The preceding comments apply to the boards of directors of public companies, those companies whose stock is actively traded. Directors of private companies—companies whose stock is owned or controlled by management or by venture capitalists— have a somewhat different role. The Frank Cavier case, at the end of this chapter, describes some of the matters to be considered by a person who has been invited to join the board of a private company.

The basic difference between a private board and a public board is that a member of a private board can be discharged by the controlling shareowner (usually the CEO) without notice. Therefore, directors are not trying to appraise the CEO, or to look for his successor. The function of directors of a private board is to assist the CEO, period. They bring expertise and experience that might not otherwise be available. They are advisors, hand holders, and sounding boards, in a more intimate way than are directors of a public company. If they are dissatisfied or uncomfortable with the way things are going, they can resign without the publicity that accompanies resignation from a public board.

Directors of private companies do, however, have the same fiduciary responsibility as directors of public companies. They can be sued by minority stockowners, creditors, disgruntled employees, or others for gross negligence or for acting in their personal interest rather than in the corporate interest. Therefore, in considering membership on a private board, don't overlook the possibility of legal liability, even if you feel a strong desire to help a friend or to tackle the challenges of an enterprise with glamorous prospects. There are, in fact, some who specifically advise against board membership in such instances.[1] They point out that an outsider can provide assistance to a small, closely held company as an advisor or member of an advisory board, rather than as a formal member of its board of directors. In this way they can avoid the legal liability associated with board membership while at the same time serving a useful role.

The owners of a private company should think very carefully about their objectives before inviting an outsider to join their board. If they seek "window dressing," then they need to make sure that the director they invite is willing to play that role—a person who understands that he is expected not to ask questions, but rather to go along with all proposals. If they misjudge the person and elect a person who expects to be actively involved in corporate affairs, the arrangement will inevitably turn out to be unsatisfactory.

If the owners are serious about having a board that will be helpful, they must be willing to spend considerable time and effort in making the relationship work. They must

- Provide information that they normally would not share with others,
- Plan and organize constructive board meetings,
- Be open-minded and willing to listen to criticism from people who are less familiar with the company than they are, and
- Create an atmosphere in which an outsider (who knows he

[1]Eugene M. Zuckert and John H. Quinn, Jr., "Small Company Advisors: Substitute for Outside Directors," *Michigan Business Review*, May 1974.

can be fired without notice) will have a feeling of genuine participation.

This is not easy, but it can be done.

BOARDS OF ACQUIRED COMPANIES

When one company acquires another, the parent sometimes agrees to retain the board of the new subsidiary. This board soon becomes a useless appendage. The parent company is the only shareowner. The subsidiary's management looks to the parent for guidance, not to the subsidiary's board of directors. When du Pont acquired Conoco in 1981, an $8+ billion transaction, du Pont initially decided to regard Conoco as a separate entity with its own board. The Conoco board was restructured to include several senior Conoco officers, several of the former outside Conoco board members, and three du Pont officers, including the chairman, Edward Jefferson, and the former board chairman and current chairman of the du Pont Finance Committee, Irving Shapiro. This board was disbanded after 18 months. Nonetheless, it served a useful purpose during the transition period. It gave the senior management of both companies time to decide how they would structure their relationships.

Once the acquisition had been accomplished, the role of the former outside Conoco board members changed dramatically. One director who served on the interim board described it as follows:

As a member of the old Conoco board, I felt a real responsibility to represent and vote for the interests of the diverse group of Conoco constituencies, primarily, of course, the shareowners. This was an obligation and a challenge that had real meaning. Being on the board after du Pont took over was entirely different. For example, as a director on that board when it came to vote, I often looked across the table at Ed Jefferson and thought, "Why am I voting? He has all the votes!" This was not by way of complaint. In fact, I think du Pont was wise to use this board for an

*interim period. However, the reality is that for an outsider, participating
on such a board is an exercise in impotency.*

CONCLUSION

The director walks a tightrope. His responsibility is to be supportive of management, but not a rubber stamp. He directs, but he does not manage. Legally, he has the ultimate responsibility for both the formulation of strategy and its implementation, but as a practical matter in most circumstances he relies on the CEO. He and his fellow directors elected the CEO, but he may later have to remove him. He is responsible for the long-run health of the company, but most of the information he receives on its performance relates to the short run. He has a legal responsibility to the shareowners, but he has a moral responsibility to employees, customers, vendors, and society as a whole. He is responsible for keeping the shareowners informed, but at the same time he should not disclose information that would be adverse to the company's best interests. He has personal goals, as does the CEO. However, the director must ensure that neither his goals nor those of the CEO overshadow their obligation to the corporation and its goals.

It's an exciting experience.

CASE
Quality Stores—Preparing For Succession

In 1983, John Kemp, a member of the board of Quality Stores, was concerned about discussions the board was having with Peter Black, Quality Stores' chairman and CEO. These discussions concerned two principal topics: planning for succession and organizational structure. Kemp was worried that the board might be giving confusing signals to Chairman Black.

Background.   Quality Stores began in 1953 as a small sporting goods store in Dallas, Texas. It grew steadily by adding and acquiring more stores, until by 1965 it had 60 units operating across the Sun Belt under the name Sports Unlimited. After 1965, Quality Stores broadened its line, first by acquiring a small chain of book stores, Books for All, and later by acquiring a chain of specialty clothing stores for young people, called Clothes for Kids. Under the continuing management of the founding group, these three chains continued to grow and prosper.

In 1970, Quality Stores went public. The founders continued as active managers, and still owned about 30 percent of the shares. By 1975, sales exceeded $500 million. The rapid expansion created management problems; although the company continued to be financially healthy, profits were not keeping pace. It also became clear that there was not, within the company, a suitable individual to become the next CEO, a person who could manage the more complex and widespread operation that Quality Stores had become. In 1978, following an extensive search, Peter Black was brought in as president and chief operating officer, with the expectation that he would, within a year or two, become chairman and CEO. At that time the two founders would withdraw from day-to-day management but would remain on the board of directors, with one of them serving as chairman.

Black, age 50, had extensive management experience as an executive vice president of a large national retail organization. He had immediate success in solving several important management problems. He brought imagination and discipline to the organization. He installed controls, set standards, and established a long-term growth strategy. After Black's initial year, in which some write-offs were taken, profits grew impressively and the company's stock responded well. The board was pleased with Black's performance, and in 1980 he was elected chairman and CEO. At that time the company had 15,000 employees and sales exceeded $750 million.

During this period the board was expanded and strengthened. Prior to 1975 it had consisted largely of insiders. By 1980 the board had nine members: the two founders, Black, and six outsiders, all with extensive management and board experience.

Succession. Shortly after Black became CEO, one of the newer board members, John Kemp, raised the issue of succession in the event that something were to happen to Black. The board asked Black for his assessment of possible candidates within the company. In February 1981 Black reported back to the board. He said that there was no one inside the company whom he would be comfortable in recommending. In his opinion, the executive vice president, James LaPlante, was an excellent administrator and operations man, but was somewhat lacking in leadership abilities. Ed Manning, the financial vice president, was an impressive young man (age 39) who was doing an outstanding job. Black said that although Manning had potential, at present he was too young and lacked line operating experience. Black added that the company had a number of fine young executives in the line organization, and in time one or more could surface as potential successors. He admitted, however, that this was not a current solution to the problem.

Following Black's report, the board went into executive session. Kemp reminded the board of the company's continuing vulnerability in the event that Black resigned or was somehow incapacitated. Moreover, the company's performance under Black's leadership was becoming widely recognized, and Kemp was concerned that Black might be hired away from Quality Stores. Although the members considered Black well compensated, they knew that he was ambitious and that he was probably receiving attractive offers from other companies. With these considerations in mind, the board decided to ask Black to retain a search firm to try to identify a suitable successor candidate from outside the company. This was done.

Several excellent, experienced candidates were interviewed. However, the best ones were all about Black's age; such people probably would not want to remain in the number two position until Black's retirement. Other candidates needed seasoning, and in that respect were not much different from some of the promising young executives currently employed by Quality Stores. Reluctantly, the board terminated the search with the succession problem still unresolved.

In January 1982, Kemp raised the succession issue again at an executive session of the board. Several board members remarked that they were highly impressed with young Manning. He was maturing, he handled himself well, and he appeared to have an excellent relationship with the line organization, even though it was his job to keep close tabs on them and, occasionally, to blow the whistle. He was, however, only 41 and still had no line experience. The board asked Black to develop an organization plan that would give Manning the line experience necessary to become CEO.

The Plan.   At a board meeting three months later, Black presented his plan. He proposed to set up an *Office of the President*, which would include both LaPlante and Manning. All line and staff functions would report to this office, except for legal and public relations, which would report directly to Black. Black's proposal also provided for a division of responsibilities between LaPlante and Manning. One of the operating divisions, Sports Unlimited, would be Manning's responsibility, and some of Manning's staff responsibilities, including corporate planning, would go to LaPlante. Manning would continue to be responsible for the finance and control functions. Black's concept was that this arrangement would expose Manning to all company-wide problems. Assigning him Sports Unlimited would give him an opportunity to demonstrate his ability as a line manager.

Board members expressed a wide range of views on Black's proposal. Some considered it unwise to have an Office of the President in which several people shared responsibilities. Others believed that giving an officer both line and staff responsibilities was a mistake. Still others wondered if it would be prudent to give Manning full responsibility for such a major portion of the company's business.

The meeting ended with no consensus. Kemp argued that it was worth a risk to give Manning some line experience. Others agreed that he needed the experience but felt that this was not the way to do it. Kemp privately wondered whether the board should become involved in organizational issues. Black, while wanting to respond to the board's wishes, was uncertain about what he should do next.

Our Comment on Quality Stores

The Quality Stores case highlights the distinction between the role of the director and that of the CEO. Kemp was clearly right in expressing his concern that there be a suitable back-up for Black. Identification of a successor is a primary board obligation. On the other hand, the board's reaction to Black's organizational proposal was tantamount to direct involvement by the board in the CEO's executive responsibility.

The Quality Stores board was currently in a vulnerable position. If Black left the company, the directors would probably have to look outside for a successor, a less than ideal solution. Kemp properly exercised his responsibility as a board member by keeping the succession issue alive. In turn, it was the board's job to press Black for a solution. Having failed to bring in a seasoned backup for Black, the board should certainly accelerate the development of internal candidates. Since Manning was the most likely person, and since his principal weakness was in line management, it was proper for the board to ask Black to structure the organization so as to provide Manning with such an opportunity. Without the board's pressure, Black might not have given this a high priority, since if he left it wouldn't be his problem; it would be the board's. (This attitude, perhaps subconscious, is not uncommon with younger, ambitious CEO's who see a long, progressively promising career ahead.)

Upon Black's presentation of his reorganization plan, the board expressed a variety of views, and questioned the proposal. Board members have every right—indeed they have an obligation—to question anything that comes before them. They should be careful to make a distinction, however, between those issues which directors decide and those within the province of the CEO. In this instance, the directors should have given Black counsel and advice, but they should have made it clear that in the end he is responsible for details of organization arrangements. Otherwise the board would not be able to hold him accountable for the results.

Moreover, the board should realize that Black is closer to the situation than they are; he is familiar with the people and knows how they can be expected to interact. In addition, individuals generally will work harder to make their own ideas work than to implement ideas that have been forced upon them. Thus, the Quality Stores board should be frank with Black but at the same time make it clear that the final decision is his—so long as the plan provides Manning the opportunity for line management experience.

Black would be wise to consider carefully the various opinions expressed by his directors. He might want to follow up with private discussions with some of them. They may have excellent ideas that Black has overlooked. Such a process frequently results in a far better decision than that originally proposed. Moreover, board members are likely to be more supportive if they realize that their views were considered. In the final analysis, however, Black must make up his own mind. It is his organization, and he must take responsibility for it.

CASE
Frank Cavier—A Private Company

In early 1975, Frank Cavier (age 66) was asked to join the board of directors of Sky-Hi Corporation, a privately held company. One of the two shareowners of Sky-Hi had been a personal friend for more than 25 years. Cavier couldn't decide whether or not to become a member of this board.

The Situation.   Sky-Hi was a fresh produce packing and marketing company, with headquarters in Orlando, Florida. In late 1974 Sky-Hi was purchased by Clu Carey (age 54) and DeWitt Wolfe (age 56) from a large conglomerate which had decided that the business did not fit its future strategy. Carey and Wolfe owned the entire company, 50 percent each. Carey, who was Cavier's friend, was involved in a variety of enterprises. He owned and operated several agricultural properties, was an investor in several more, had interests in a number of real estate ventures, and acted as a consultant and broker in trading large agricultural properties. While Carey and Cavier had known one another for many years, they had never had any actual business dealings. Cavier regarded Carey as an interesting and stimulating person, and whenever they were together they talked a good deal about business matters.

Wolfe was semi-retired, having sold out his interest in a successful electronics firm which he had founded. He owned extensive farming properties in Florida, but he did not actively manage them. Wolfe and Carey had come to know each other well; they lived in the same area and had some business interests in common. Both Wolfe and Carey had substantial net worths, which Cavier guessed to be in the eight-figure neighborhood. Cavier, who lived in Atlanta, Georgia, had met Wolfe only a few times but was favorably impressed with him; he seemed like a "good guy."

Cavier had recently retired. During the middle of his career, he had been the CEO of a medium-size industrial firm. Subsequently, he was an officer of a regional investment banking firm. He had a good reputation in the business community, both in Atlanta and elsewhere. While not particularly wealthy, he was comfortably well-off, in good health, and eager to remain active.

He enjoyed the associations that he maintained with business friends. He was still on the boards of five publicly held major corporations. In anticipation of retirement, he had also become involved in several nonprofit, public-service activities in Atlanta, including a hospital board, a community youth group, and others. A few months after retirement he was surprised at how busy he was.

The Proposal. The Sky-Hi board, which Cavier was invited to join, consisted of Carey, Wolfe, and their attorney. Since Cavier and Wolfe owned all the stock, this board fulfilled the necessary legal corporate requirements. When Carey approached Cavier to sound him out about joining the Sky-Hi board, Cavier asked why he wanted any more people on the board. Why not keep it as simple as possible? Carey replied that both he and Wolfe thought Cavier could be useful to Sky-Hi. Carey said he didn't want to become personally involved in day-to-day management; he was primarily interested in expanding Sky-Hi by adding more packing houses and acquiring new properties. Wolfe, on the other hand had considerable management experience, but he was unfamiliar with the marketing and management issues in a company like Sky-Hi. Moreover, Wolfe had retired once, and he was not anxious to take on another long-term, full-time management job. While Sky-Hi had a management in place, both Carey and Wolfe believed it needed considerable revamping and tightening.

It was in these areas of general management and company strategy that Carey said Cavier could be helpful. Carey and Wolfe wanted to bounce ideas and plans off Cavier, get his frank opinions, and have him available for advice. They might meet four to six times a year—whenever it was convenient—and they could do it in either Orlando or Atlanta. They would plan to pay a board meeting fee of $1,000 for each meeting if agreeable to Cavier.

Carey gave Cavier financial statements and literature on Sky-Hi, and Cavier found them quite interesting. Sky-Hi owned a number of produce packing plants in Florida and several in California. It also owned some orchards, but it purchased most of its fruit and other produce from local growers, usually under some type of contractual agreement. Sky-Hi had several types of marketing arrangements, including selling directly to importers in Japan and Europe, and marketing in the United States through cooperative marketing groups. Wolfe and Carey believed that significant improvements could be made in marketing.

The company was financially sound, and there was no significant pending litigation. The owners were willing to make additional investments in Sky-Hi in order to see it grow. Carey told Cavier that both he and Wolfe were in 100 percent agreement on asking him to join their board, and although Cavier didn't know Wolfe well, Carey could vouch for his integrity, character, and ability.

At the conclusion of this meeting, Carey reminded Cavier of their long and friendly relationship and stated that he valued their friendship greatly. He added that he admired Cavier's sense of perspective and his judgment, and that it would be a lot of fun to work together. Moreover, who could tell what might develop later on in terms of other projects in which they might have mutual interests?

Cavier's Considerations. Cavier reacted with pleasure to Carey's invitation. He really liked the guy, they got along well, and discussing business matters with him was stimulating. Moreover, the Sky-Hi situation was interesting. It would be something new for Cavier, and it didn't appear that the directorship would constitute a burden either in terms of time or of responsibility. And an affiliation such as Carey proposed certainly would not hurt Cavier's reputation or status. Finally, while the money he would receive as a board member was not especially significant, Cavier was tempted by the possibility of future business relationships with Carey, Wolfe, or both.

There were some negatives, however. First, there was the possible liability. As a director, his legal liabilities would be identical with Carey's and Wolfe's. Although there would be the usual indemnities and director's liability insurance, why should he subject himself to this exposure when Carey and Wolfe could get the same kind of advice from him as a consultant? Did they want him as a director just so they could use his name? Cavier didn't think this was Carey's motive, although he realized that his name as a director would be an asset to Sky-Hi Corporation.

The Sky-Hi directorship would not conflict with any of his other directorships. However, he realized that there would be many differences between serving on the Sky-Hi board and being on his other boards. In both instances he would be serving the shareowners; however, he could be dismissed as a board member from Sky-Hi almost on a moment's notice. Carey, Wolfe and their attorney could hold a special shareowners' meeting at any time, and vote him out. While Cavier didn't think this would happen, the mere possibility made this role different from his other directorships. In the publicly held companies, Cavier felt that he represented the interests of the shareowners and other constituencies. Moreover, he could very likely look forward to being reelected as a director until retirement. By contrast, in Sky-Hi he would be serving strictly for the owners and at their whim.

Cavier also wondered whether he might find himself in an awkward position between Wolfe and Carey. He knew it was not uncommon for partners to disagree, and as a third party he might find himself in the middle of a potentially messy situation. This would take the fun out of it.

This dilemma brought to mind the experience of Frank Marshall, a friend who had been the sole outside member of the board of a small, highly successful, family-owned company. Marshall had been asked to join that board because he was a long-standing friend of the family members, and they had said they wanted his help and advice. As it turned out, the owners were reluctant to share any but the most minimal financial and operating information with the board. All other information, including plans and projections, was considered personal and private. Without this kind of background information, Marshall found it impossible to conduct meaningful discussions on company issues. The situation became frustrating. Toward the end, his only activity as a director was to become involved in unpleasant family disagreements over how the business was being run. Marshall finally resigned in disgust. He told Cavier that never again would he consider membership on the board of a privately held company.

Cavier was unsure what to decide. He believed that if Carey and Wolfe were sincere about creating a true board relationship, then he could enjoy his participation while being helpful to them. Although he knew very little about Sky-Hi's business, he could help the two owners with such broad corporate issues as strategy, organization, financing, and possibly going public. He would enjoy this. On the other hand, with ownership so concentrated, he wondered if there would be an opportunity to make a meaningful contribution. In addition there was always the risk of destroying a good friendship. Add to these considerations the liability exposure and the minimal financial remuneration, and Cavier wondered if he would be wise to accept Carey's invitation.

What Happened. In the end Cavier decided to accept. Another business person whom Cavier knew well also joined the board. Carey and Wolfe took the board seriously, and it functioned effectively. They provided the two outsiders with all relevant information on Sky-Hi's operations, and they conducted serious and well-prepared board meetings. Important issues were thoroughly reviewed at these meetings, and Cavier believed that the board was helpful in providing a perspective, especially on matters of policy and organization. At a minimum, the two outside directors made it possible for Carey and Wolfe to have critical and objective discussions on their evolving policies and programs. In addition, Carey frequently telephoned or visited Cavier in Atlanta to bring him up to date and to talk about company matters.

Under Carey's and Wolfe's direction, numerous changes were made in the company. Top management was restructured, new marketing programs were initiated, and several companies were acquired. These changes greatly improved Sky-Hi's profitability, and its outlook for continued growth was promising. Cavier enjoyed the association, in part because of the personal relationships, but also because he believed that he was making a useful contribution. He was proud of the company's success.

In 1982, Carey and Wolfe accepted an offer to merge Sky-Hi into an international corporation interested in the fresh produce business. They received stock in the acquiring company worth seven times their original investment.

Our Comment on the Frank Cavier Case

The Cavier case illustrates some of the significant differences between directorship of privately held and publicly held companies. Whether or not the board of a privately held company can be useful depends largely on the owners. They can make it work—or turn it into a farce. Sky-Hi's board was effective because Carey and Wolfe treated it seriously and respected the role of the outsiders, although they had no legal obligation to do so. They involved Cavier and the second outside director in the company's real issues by encouraging them to participate and by making them feel part of the team. This attitude made the two outside directors useful board members, and also gave them a sense of accomplishment that probably exceeded any monetary considerations.

In the case of Frank Marshall, Cavier's friend, the board was a useless fiction. The family owners failed to understand the true role of a board of directors; they tried to use the outside director to help resolve family arguments. By witholding information and by avoiding any serious discussion of business issues, they eliminated any possibility of having a useful board. The family members received no help from their board and lost a friend in the process. Unfortunately, Marshall's experience is not uncommon. Cavier was fortunate.

3

The Role of the Chairman–CEO

The chairman–CEO holds the key to determining the board's effectiveness. The way he views the role of the board and his relationship with board members determines in large measure how well the board functions. A host of other activities under his control—including the way he organizes and conducts meetings, and the information he chooses to provide to board members—can also influence the effectiveness of the board. This chapter addresses the role of the CEO as board chairman, and suggests ways in which the CEO can help make the board useful and constructive. In the discussion that follows, we assume (except when otherwise noted) that the CEO is also chairman of the board.

THE CEO'S ATTITUDE

Various CEOs have widely differing perceptions of the role of their boards. Some CEOs regard the board as an unfortunate, but necessary, legal nuisance. Other CEOs see the board as the legitimate instrument of corporate governance to which they are accountable; they deal with it seriously and responsibly. With a CEO of the former type, the board is almost certain to be weak and ineffective. With the latter, the board is likely to be strong and useful. The CEO's view of the role of his board and the way in which he chooses to relate to the board has a major impact on the board's effectiveness.

The CEO who truly wants a strong, effective board usually has a clear sense of his role vis-à-vis the board. While exercising leadership, he also makes it apparent that he is accountable to the board. This does not imply a demeaning or subservient relationship, but is simply a recognition by the CEO that the governing process starts with the board. In both a formal and legal sense, the CEO serves at the pleasure of, and is accountable to, the board. The CEO who forgets this does so at some risk. The successful and independent persons who compose a good board do not appreciate a CEO who appears to take them for granted, or who seems not to acknowledge his accountability to them. This type of attitude on the part of a CEO does not help to create a constructive board–CEO relationship.

There are, of course, a number of CEOs overseeing successful companies whose style is to dominate their organizations—management as well as the board. It would be a good guess that these managers tend to view their boards as necessary nuisances and window dressing. Strong, successful, and independent persons tend not to be interested in serving on such boards. Consequently, these boards are unlikely to be particularly effective.

A problem that frequently arises with a domineering CEO is the selection of a successor and the orderly transition of authority and leadership. Cases in point, judging from statements in the business press, might be Armand Hammer of Occidental, Harold Geneen of ITT, and Harry Gray of United Technologies. In each instance there either is, or was, a succession problem.

A CEO who recognizes the governing role of the board and considers himself accountable to it will work with his directors on the all-important task of his succession. An overly domineering CEO may try to perpetuate his own power, create turmoil within the organization so there is not a suitable successor, and otherwise conduct himself so as to frustrate the legitimate interests of the board. Who would want to serve on a board with this kind of leadership?

It is interesting to note that several years after retiring from ITT, Harold Geneen expressed the view (September 17, 1984, issue of *Fortune*) that boards are largely impotent and ineffective; are unable to protect the shareowners' interests; meekly follow the chairman's lead; and do so because of the extravagant fees and perks they receive, largess for which they should feel indebted to the chairman. Judging from the legends surrounding Geneen's management style, one wonders about the extent to which he tolerated divergent views from his board; whether he wanted strong, independent-minded persons on his board, and whether or not he considered himself as being truly accountable to the board. We can only speculate on such matters.

TRUST

Those familiar with boards will agree that an effective board begins with a constructive relationship and mutual trust between the CEO and the outside board members. The board must—repeat *must*—believe beyond any question that the CEO is completely trustworthy, that he provides the board with every bit of information it wants and needs, accurately and promptly, and that nothing is being, or ever would be, withheld. Any suspicion on the part of the board that the CEO is "playing games," is being less than forthright in providing information, or is slanting it to support a preconceived position, is destructive of the absolute trust essential to this relationship.

The other side of this coin is that the CEO must be convinced that he has the board's support. He should not be in a position to suspect, for example, that board members are meeting privately to question his actions, or that they are plotting to make a change.

Numerous cases throughout this book illustrate the importance of this sense of trust. In the Telemix case (Chapter 4) the CEO's relationship with the board deteriorated as the board lost confidence in the CEO's reports on projected earnings. Finally, after the board replaced the CEO, a board member commented, "I don't think he was consciously lying to us, but . . . ." Obviously, there was a loss of confidence and trust without which there could be no effective working relationship.

The Cleary Company case (Chapter 1) describes the situation in which a director voted against a proposal recommended by management. Some CEOs become nearly paranoid over a director's "no" vote, as if it were a symbol of "no confidence." If there is a constructive trusting relationship, an occasional "no" vote will be taken for what it is—an honest difference of opinion between reasonable people. Furthermore, if the CEO is upset by a negative vote, it suggests that he might be insecure in his relationship with the board. The needed sense of trust does not exist.

How is this sense of trust and confidence developed and maintained? The most natural way is for it to evolve over a period of time as the board and the executive work closely together. One of the important reasons for having a CEO's probable successor serve on the board, in fact, is to provide an opportunity for this sense of trust to develop and mature.

The CEO who is also chairman of the board is the key person in the CEO–board relationship. What can the CEO do to preserve or enhance this relationship?

SUGGESTIONS FOR CHAIRMAN–CEOs

1. *Information.* Make sure your board has all the information it wants and needs. A board cannot function in an information vacuum. Don't overkill, but be sensitive to what various board members want and then provide it. For example, if a board member asks a question at a board meeting and the information is not immediately available, make sure that it is mailed as soon as possible following the meeting. Ask the board from time to time about the adequacy of the information being provided. Be alert to their suggestions and tailor board materials and presentations to their wishes—not to what you think they should have.

2. *No surprises.* Avoid surprising your board—unless, of course, you can't help it, as in the case of an unfriendly tender offer. Above all, never let a board member learn for the first time about an important company development by reading about it in the newspaper. Advise him ahead of time—by telephone if necessary.

With regard to decisions the board must make on major issues, most of the time, with some forethought, you can lay the groundwork and prepare your board ahead of time. For example, if you are planning to make a significant organizational change, tell the board a month or two ahead of time about your ideas; why a change is needed; what you expect to accomplish; and who might be involved. Solicit advice from the board, either at the meeting or privately. Then, when you ask them to approve your new organization plan, they are likely to be comfortable with it and support it. And who knows? A board member might even have a useful suggestion for you.

Such an approach should be used for all major issues you want the board to address—acquisitions, divestitures, new financing, changes in corporate strategy, and so on. Your board will respond constructively if you have consulted them in advance, solicited their thoughts, and allowed them time to reflect on the decision they will be asked to make. With this approach, you let your directors know that you don't take them for granted and that you respect their views. Conversely, if you spring a big decision on them without advance notice or preparation, you are saying that you consider them to be nothing more than a rubber stamp. No board member appreciates this—and it can't help but impair your relationship.

3. *Informal Activities.* In Chapter 2 we pointed out the importance of having informal and social activities outside the

board room. The initiative for these must come from you, the
CEO. If you don't plan and organize such occasions, they will
not take place, and you will miss a wonderful opportunity to
foster good board relationships. The nature of your board, the
kind of business you are in, the resources you have available,
and your own style will determine the type and frequency of
the events appropriate for your board. Get them out of the
board room, take them on plant tours, arrange for them to play
golf with your senior executives, occasionally involve spouses
in social events—the list is limited only by your imagination.
These activities will enhance the CEO–board relationship, and
you will very likely gain a more productive board. But remember, this depends on you—you must be the initiator.

4. *Board Review.* We suggested earlier that you ask your
board members whether they are receiving all the information
they want. Consider expanding on this idea by asking board
members for suggestions as to how you, the chairman, can help
make board meetings optimally productive. Are there enough—
or too many—meetings? Are the right topics being addressed?
Are the presentations clear, too long, too short? Is there enough
time for discussion? How about plant tours and visits? Do
members have sufficient contact with senior executives who
are not on the board? How about the board's composition?
When you open up such subjects, you may be surprised by
what you hear. You won't be able to respond to all of the suggestions, but if you listen carefully, you will learn a lot. We
know of one chairman who asked a senior director to solicit
the views of his fellow directors and report to him without
revealing the source of individual suggestions. This turned out
to be a constructive process for all concerned.

5. *Preparation.* Board meetings should be well prepared, but
this is not always the case. People who serve on several boards
can quickly note the difference that good preparation makes.
Some boards get a lot of work done in a reasonable period of
time and still have adequate time for discussion. Other boards
run through presentation after presentation, leaving no time

for discussion, and this causes frustration. Still others ramble on endlessly, almost like a "bull-session," accomplishing little. Thoughtful, careful preparation makes the difference. It starts with the agenda. Are the essentials included—and the trivia left out? Are the presentations rehearsed and timed? Is there time for discussion? Every meeting is different, but you, as chairman, are responsible for the careful planning of both con-tent and format so the board will feel that its time is well spent.

Some of the foregoing suggestions for CEOs may appear to be trivial. Our observation is, however, that in many instances fail-ure to pay attention to these matters adversely affects the all-important CEO–board relationship, and consequently the board's effectiveness.

RELATIONSHIP PROBLEMS

At the end of this chapter there are two cases, Menlo Corpora-tion and Acme Energy, which depict problems in the relation-ship between a CEO and the board.

A common criticism of some boards of directors is that they are passive, slow to challenge the CEO, and act merely as rubber stamps. Unfortunately, this is an accurate characterization of some boards. Even when there is a good, constructive relation-ship between the board and the CEO, it is sometimes difficult to get sensitive issues out in the open. Individual directors may be uncomfortable about the course the company is taking, but they may also be reluctant to make their concerns known. Moreover, CEOs, who usually are strong, confident people, may be highly sensitive to what they interpret as criticism. Accordingly, they may either avoid discussion of controversial issues or, when they do discuss them, they may give the impression that their position is obviously the right one, and that further discussion is not wel-come.

The good CEO creates an environment that encourages debate and discussion within the board. He is a good listener. Likewise, the effective director will manage his relations with the CEO so he can raise controversial matters with the minimum likelihood of offending the CEO. The essence of an effective board is active, candid interaction among all participants. It is the responsibility of both the CEO and the directors to develop an atmosphere which encourages wide and frank participation. Many corporate boards have some distance to go to achieve this objective.

CEOs WHO ARE NOT CHAIRMEN

In this book we usually assume that the CEO is also the chairman of the board. Although this is typically the case, there are numerous instances of board chairmen who are not CEOs. Moreover, there are many variations within this arrangement. The title of chairman is sometimes largely honorary—recognition of being a company founder or long-serving officer and director. Under the circumstances, the chairman might simply open and close the board meetings, leaving the actual conduct of the meetings to the president and CEO. Other chairmen are partially active, representing the company's interests, for example, to the government or to its industry. In some instances, the chairman is a full-time executive who shares top management duties with the president-CEO. Finally, there are chairmen who concentrate their activities solely on the governance issues, avoiding involvement in executive management, which is the province of the president-CEO.[1]

The reason the positions of chairman and CEO are usually combined is that this provides a single focal point for company leadership. There is never any question about who the boss is or who is responsible. This is an important issue. There are unfortunate examples of chairmen–CEOs who relinquish their role and title of CEO to a president and then forget they are no longer

[1]An excellent discussion of this arrangement is in "Corporate Governance: The Other Side of the Coin," by Kenneth N. Dayton (*Harvard Business Review*, January–February, 1984).

running the show. This is guaranteed to produce chaos both within the organization and in relationships with the board.

In such a situation, the board needs to exercise caution in establishing an arrangement in which the roles of chairman and CEO are separated. There must be a clear understanding of respective responsibilities, and these must be carefully observed. Moreover, there must be unusually good "chemistry" between the two individuals. If the relationship is competitive or if there are ego problems, a division of responsibility is not likely to work.

A mentor relationship between a chairman and a CEO can be the basis of an effective team. A good example is at Hewlett-Packard, where John Young became president and CEO in 1978, at age 46, while the founders, David Packard and William Hewlett, continued as chairman and vice-chairman, respectively. Less common are situations in which the chairman and CEO share management responsibilities. This was done successfully for a number of years at the McKesson Corporation, with Neil Harlan as full-time chairman and Thomas Drohan as president and CEO. Harlan had the principal responsibility for finance, planning, and external affairs, while Drohan concentrated on corporate operations. An even less common arrangement is at Dayton-Hudson, where a clear distinction is made between the functions of governance and executive management. It is Dayton-Hudson's view that one person (a chairman–CEO) cannot perform both functions effectively. Consequently, they assign the governing role to the full-time chairman and the management role to the president and CEO. The concept is well thought out, and warrants consideration. However, given the understandable propensity of CEOs to retain their positions of power, we would not expect to see a rush toward the Dayton-Hudson arrangement.

CONCLUSION

The CEO plays the key role in determining the board's effectiveness. If he perceives his board as significant to the corporation's governance and policy-making processes, the board is likely to be productive. If, on the other hand, he looks upon his board as a necessary nuisance, it will probably be ineffective.

A good board will select a CEO in whom it has full confidence and who has demonstrated qualities of leadership that can make an organization work effectively together. The CEO, in turn, will pay particular attention to his relationship with his board. What he does in his interactions with the directors will determine, to a considerable degree, the effectiveness of that board.

CASE
Acme Energy Company—From Success to Disappointment

Without question, Alden Ames was a seasoned, successful, and experienced businessman. When he formed Acme Energy Company, he was 54 years old and at the height of his career. Earlier he had started his own company, built it up, and sold it on very favorable terms. Later he acquired control of another company, expanding it through the acquisition of complementary units and ultimately merging it into a large, financially successful corporation. More recently, he and a prominent investment bank purchased Acme Energy, a successful privately owned company. The investment bank acquired 75 percent of Acme's equity, while Ames bought the remaining 25 percent. It was the intent of the investment bank to hold its interest for a few years and, when the time was right, to have the company go public and to sell all or a major portion of its interest.

Under Ames's leadership, Acme's business expanded rapidly. Moreover, with the investment bank's assistance, a number of smaller companies compatible with Acme's business were acquired. Everything worked extremely well, and within two years the company went public. The shares were actively traded and were soon selling at a premium over the issue price. All indications were that Ames was on his way to another big success.

From the beginning, Ames was determined to have a good

board and to operate his company in the best tradition of a public company. He attracted a group of outstanding business people to serve on Acme's board, most of whom had known Ames for some time and who admired both his accomplishments and his capabilities. Several were close personal friends.

Shortly after the company went public, Ames embarked on an expanded acquisition program. He felt that the time was ripe, and because Acme's stock was favorably priced, he could rapidly expand his company by acquiring other companies on terms that would be advantageous to Acme's shareowners. He negotiated substantial bank loans for Acme, both to finance its expanding operations and to make acquisitions for cash. The company became highly leveraged.

During the course of this expansion program, several directors expressed concern over the pace at which acquisitions were being made. It also seemed that some of the acquired companies did not follow any particular strategic pattern. They wondered how such a disparate group of organizations, brought together so rapidly, could be managed effectively. Ames seemed to respect the views of these members of his board, and he carefully and thoroughly responded to their questions. In fact, some board members felt overwhelmed by the persuasive reasoning and the obvious sincerity, as well as the intensity, of Ames' feelings. The energy business was booming, and Acme was in an ideal position to obtain for itself a leadership position if it moved quickly and decisively. Given Ames' record of success and the strength of his feelings, it seemed difficult to challenge his position—much less to change his mind.

By 1980 the energy industry began to suffer from an oversupply and weakening prices. Most of Acme's businesses were quite vulnerable to this economic downturn, and Acme Energy's fortunes were soon reversed. Trouble seemed to crop up everywhere. Divisions that had been acquired turned out not to be as strong as expected, managers were unable to cope with new problems, and Acme's senior management, while competent, was incapable of dealing with all the fires that sprang up. Earnings turned to losses and bank borrowings became excessive. To make a long story short, Acme was forced to seek a merger with a much stronger company, but it did so at considerable loss to its shareowners.

Our Comment on Acme Energy Company

What went wrong? Was the board at fault? If so, what could or should a board member have done to prevent Acme's demise?

Ames was a highly successful businessman, with a record of profitable ventures and a considerable personal fortune. An important inducement to Acme's shareowners was to have a "piece of the action" that was sure to be generated by this exceptional individual. Acme's early growth and the rise in the price of its stock certainly indicated that Ames was on his way to producing another winner. Under these circumstances, a board member might understandably be reluctant to voice negative opinions about Ames' activities. When events took a turn for the worse, one could argue that this was the time for the board to give Ames encouragement and support. He was a vigorous, brilliant man who had successfully overcome other difficult situations. Without the benefit of hindsight, who was to say that he wouldn't do it again? This is when a CEO most needs the help and support of his board—not carping criticisms.

It should be remembered that Ames was persuasive in his responses to the board's questions. In fact, it appears that he had "all the answers" and that there was not much likelihood of changing his mind. Moreover, by being too persistent, a director might be seen as "troublesome" and could even create strained relationships within the board.

On the other hand, if a board member was seriously concerned with the way Ames was managing Acme Energy, we believe that he had an obligation to bring his views to the board's attention and to stimulate debate on the issues. One way to do this would be for the concerned director to discuss his views informally with one or more of his fellow directors. If they had similar concerns, a nucleus of a consensus might develop, which in turn would at least support bringing up the issue for consideration by the full board. Of course, given Ames's determination and confidence, one questions whether there was any chance of changing the company's direction. Nevertheless, if a director has a deeply held conviction, he should at least make an effort to bring the matter before the full board. However, here is where his skills are important. Some people have the ability to win the support of their colleagues and to present their views in a quiet, convincing way, without being abrasive or combative. Other people can hardly avoid a confrontation. The effective director takes the time to prepare his position, presents it skillfully, and has the patience to endure the discussion. This takes considerable ability.

This case also underscores the fact of life that it is not always possible to succeed. The system does not guarantee success. There is risk in being in business, and there is risk in being a director. Perhaps, given the change in the market, there was no reasonable way for Acme—or its management and board—to avoid trouble. One successful CEO commented after reading this case: "There but for the grace of God go I—and my board of directors."

CASE
Menlo Corporation—A Frustrated Board Member

Ernest Ace had a distinguished business career. His name would be immediately recognized by almost any business group. He had recently retired as chairman and CEO of a prominent firm, and he served on the boards of several major U.S. corporations. In 1983 he had been on the Menlo Corporation board for ten years, and he was, by years of service, its senior member. He was scheduled to retire from the Menlo board in two years, at age 72, in compliance with the board's mandatory retirement policy.

Menlo was a well-known company, with 1983 sales exceeding

$4 billion. Its board included several active CEOs of other companies, who were close personal friends of one another and of Menlo's Chairman. They were all members of the Business Council, and they frequently participated together in both business and social occasions. Because of their status and relationship with the chairman, they tended to exercise considerable influence at board meetings.

In 1983 Ace became concerned about Menlo's lack of progress in making arrangements for succession. The chairman and CEO, Martin Fox, was 63 years old, and the company had a mandatory retirement age, for executives, of 65. Fox had told the board that there were two, possibly three, potential candidates to succeed him, but that each needed broader experience and further testing before he would feel comfortable in making a recommendation to the board. Fox also told the board that he was working on a plan to provide the necessary experience and challenges to these men so at least one—if not more—would be prepared at the time of his retirement.

Ace initiated a discussion on this subject at several board meetings, but each time Fox had a reason for not having implemented a plan to provide the candidates with the experience they needed. Moreover, in a subtle way he made it clear that he did not appreciate being pressed on this subject. Ace's concern built until it reached the point where he privately contacted several other board members. In each case these men said they were not overly concerned, and that they were totally confident that the chairman knew what he was doing. After all, he had made a commitment to the board, and it wouldn't really be helpful to bother him further about the matter.

This did not satisfy Ace. He was afraid that Fox was not really addressing the issue and that he was putting off making some hard choices. Moreover, he felt that the CEOs on the board were reluctant to speak up to Fox, as it would be awkward because he was a close personal friend. Ace saw this group as something of a "CEO's Protective Association," and he was puzzled about how to proceed. He was chairman of the audit committee, but that was not an appropriate platform from which to press this issue. Succession was considered a full-board matter. Ace was afraid that he had already strained his relationship with Fox and was reluctant to create more of a schism.

Ace also had some misgivings regarding the selection of future directors. In the past, this process was typically handled by Fox with little involvement by, or discussion with, the outside board members. In fact, Ace could not recall any candidate suggested by Fox who did not almost automatically become a board member. It was not that Ace considered Fox to be overly domineering—it was more that most of the other board members didn't seem concerned. What bothered Ace most was that there was no process which made it possible, or comfortable, for outside board members to become involved in the selection of new directors. These two matters—succession and selection of future board members—were considered by Ace to be vital to the long-term interests of Menlo's shareowners.

Sensing that Fox was already annoyed with him, Ace wondered how he might best initiate some action to deal with the issues of succession and the selection of directors.

Our Comment on Menlo Corporation

Ace is obviously frustrated. He sees his relationship with Fox deteriorating, and this in turn inhibits him from pressing the succession and board selection issues. Moreover, he can't seem to get others on the board to share his concern and to help persuade Fox to take action.

From the facts available, we conclude that Ace's concerns are probably legitimate. However, we are even more concerned about the relationship between Ace and Fox. When a board member feels he cannot effectively communicate with the CEO, or the CEO isn't listening or doesn't care to listen, there is a problem. Ace cannot be a really effective board member, much less have a constructive influence on the succession and board selection issues, until his relationship with Fox is improved, or at least clarified.

Then again, Ace might just be a troublemaker trying to create dissension on the board or to make life difficult for Fox. However, he has been on the board for ten years and is the senior director. It seems more likely that he is trying to resolve these issues before he retires.

In either event, we think it would be wise for Fox to initiate a quiet, private, and open-ended meeting with Ace; to give Ace the opportunity to express his views—thoroughly and completely. In turn, Fox should be open and candid with Ace. If there is to be disagreement, it is better that it be in the open.

However, we suspect that Ace feels he cannot wait for an invitation from Fox, because it may never materialize. Furthermore, it doesn't appear that his fellow directors can be counted on for help. Ace should arrange a meeting with Fox to express his views and concerns. An effective director will be able to do this firmly, objectively, and diplomatically. Ace might suggest that Fox periodically bring the board up to date on progress being made in the matter of succession. With respect to Ace's concern about new board members, he might comment that having a nominating committee would be useful.

Having had this discussion, Ace should probably not expect Fox to make an immediate 180 degree turn. He should, however, expect an improved relationship with Fox so that Fox will become more responsive on both issues. Hopefully, Fox will accept Ace's suggestions, though perhaps in his own way. If he does, Ace has demonstrated that he is truly an effective director.

4

Dealing with Crises

A board can function for years without ever having to deal with a crisis. But when a crisis does occur, a board experiences extreme pressure, and normal procedures are usually inadequate. While crises can take many and sometimes unexpected forms, the two that occur most frequently are: (1) having to replace the chief executive officer and (2) receiving an unfriendly takeover offer.

Dealing with these crises often means making unpleasant and controversial decisions. An effective board, however, will face up to its responsibilities and make the hard decisions. Some boards have been justifiably criticized for shirking this responsibility. One purpose of this chapter is to focus attention on the board's critical role in dealing with crises.

As we pointed out in Chapter 2, much of a director's normal responsibility helps to prepare him for dealing with crises. He learns about the company, its operations, its key executives, its strengths and weaknesses. He learns about the industry and the competition, and he forms judgments about the company's potential. He also sizes up his colleagues on the board. Who are the leaders, who the followers, and what sorts of arguments are likely to be persuasive with each? All of this background and knowledge is important and helps a director to deal with a crisis more successfully.

REPLACING THE CHIEF EXECUTIVE OFFICER

A prime duty of the board is to select the CEO. Under normal circumstances, as we've discussed, the board expects the CEO to develop a suitable successor so that there will be a smooth transition, either at his retirement or in case of illness or accident. Sometimes, however, the transition does not proceed according to plan. The CEO may become incapacitated before a successor has been identified. Or the company's performance may deteriorate to the point where the board believes it necessary to replace the CEO. Both situations are traumatic.

Succession Problems

A dramatic succession crisis occurred in 1984 at United Technologies. Harry Gray, chairman and CEO, although reaching retirement age in November 1984, had arranged with his board to remain as CEO until the end of 1985. The clear expectation was that the president, Robert Carlson, would be his successor. In September 1984, Carlson suddenly resigned. According to press reports, Gray was reluctant to relinquish his powers as CEO, and some suspected that he had engineered Carlson's resignation. The board was in a difficult position with respect to selecting a new CEO. In addition, Carlson's resignation further strained the board's relationship with Gray. In October, Robert Daniell, the senior vice president, was named president and chief operating officer. Daniell's experience was limited, and observers suggested that he would require several years in that job to qualify as Gray's replacement. This unfortunate episode seemed to have become a test of power between the board and Gray.

The directors obviously had the legal authority to force Gray's resignation. Nevertheless, they were dealing with a delicate situation. Most people felt that Gray had done a splendid job at United Technologies. Under his leadership, the company's financial performance had dramatically improved, and this was reflected in the stock price. How would the financial community react if the board were to dismiss Gray and install a new, untested chairman and CEO? How would the organization react? What would be the attitude of the U.S. Department of Defense, United Technologies' largest customer? On the other hand, would it be healthy for the board to knuckle under to Gray and allow him to remain? For how long? Can a board in this situation afford to be passive and acquiescent? These are but a few of the questions that faced the board of United Technologies in late 1984.

A year later, October 1985, it was announced that Daniell would become CEO on January 1, 1986, with Gray remaining chairman and also chairman of a newly formed finance committee. Speculation continued as to whether Gray really was turning the leadership of the company over to Daniell. One observer was quoted as saying: "The way I see it, Bob will pedal and Harry will steer." It would appear that the board will continue to play a role in the orderly transition of leadership at United Technologies.

In grappling with questions concerning the CEO, outside board members must function without their normal board leadership. Who calls the meetings? Who sets the agenda? Who presides? In these situations an informal leadership pattern must quickly emerge. In fact, the ability to become organized under these circumstances is an important test for outside board members. Can they agree on an informal modus operandi? Or will they simply drift along with individual board members hoping either that the problem will go away or that someone else will step up and do something?

While the United Technologies situation was dramatic and became the subject of considerable press comment (much of it gossip), it is by no means unique. Even in what appear to be smooth and routine transfers of executive authority, there are often sensitive and tension-filled moments for the board. Although not all successions involve crises, that's what they can become if not properly managed.

If the outgoing CEO remains on the board, the outside board members often have to protect the new CEO from undue encroachment by the retired CEO. This requires delicate handling. There can be bruised feelings on the part of one or more executives who were passed over. Here again outside board members can sometimes help to bridge a sensitive situation—but their involvement must not interfere with the new CEO's authority. If a new CEO is brought in from the outside, the outside board members must not only agree on the decision but also demonstrate to the organization their clear and wholehearted support for the new person. The point is that the directors—especially the outsiders—play an important role in the orderly transfer of executive responsibility.

Firing the CEO

Even more difficult to deal with than a succession problem is the replacement of a CEO whose performance is considered unsatisfactory. A major criticism of some boards is that they fail to take timely action when it becomes clear that the CEO should be replaced. We believe there is considerable justification for such criticism. However, it is much easier for an outside observer to be critical than it is to be in the shoes of the directors who are faced with this decision. These are some of the toughest, as well as the most important, decisions directors are called on to make.

The decision to replace a CEO is subjective and usually emotional. Sometimes there are compelling reasons for taking action—for example, when the CEO has become an alcoholic and has seriously embarrassed the company, or when his corporate performance has dramatically deteriorated. In most instances, however, the case is not so clear. Earnings may not have kept pace with industry leaders because the board discouraged management from assuming additional debt that would have enabled the company to expand. Or perhaps a major acquisition that the board supported did not work out, resulting in a serious problem. In such instances it is not obvious that the CEO is solely at fault and should be replaced.

There are, however, several important signals that a board should be alert to in evaluating the CEO's capabilities to continue his leadership:

1. Loss of confidence in the CEO. If a significant number of directors have lost confidence in, or no longer trust, the CEO, he should be replaced.

2. Steady deterioration in corporate results. In most instances, this means that earnings seriously lag industry norms for a number of years, without a defensible explanation. This problem is usually accompanied by the consistent failure to meet projections. The board must act before it is too late.

3. Organizational instability. If the CEO consistently has problems retaining qualified senior executives, he probably should be replaced.

It is one thing for board members to begin to doubt the CEO's capabilities, but it is quite another thing for them to muster up the courage and consensus needed to take action. In most instances, replacing the CEO becomes an emotional issue. The CEO and the outside directors have usually worked together for some time and are good, if not close, friends. For the CEO, dismissal is a totally catastrophic event. It is, therefore, understandable that directors have great difficulty in bringing themselves to take action which will probably destroy the career of a business associate. This is unquestionably the principal reason that boards fail to replace unsatisfactory CEOs.

Replacing the CEO is a disagreeable task that precipitates a crisis not only for the board but for the entire organization. Furthermore, when it happens, the board must be prepared to announce a successor and to deal with the problems inherent in the transfer of executive authority. Such action puts a major bur-

den on the outside directors, and it is little wonder that they tend
to avoid these obligations. Yet this is their responsibility and ultimate obligation to the shareowners and to the other constituencies of the corporation. The conscientious director understands his responsibilities and is prepared to take action, as
disagreeable as it may be, when circumstances dictate.

UNFRIENDLY TAKEOVERS

Another type of crisis event is the hostile or unfriendly takeover
attempt. The board of the target company is in a highly stressful
situation. Decisions vital to the company's future (even its continued existence) must be made in circumstances where emotions are high, vested interests are at stake, and advice is often
conflicting. The business press reports the daily dramatic developments of offers and counteroffers, tactics and strategies, as
each side in the struggle seeks to gain an advantage. These are
truly crisis episodes and a severe test of a board's ability and
durability. Unfortunately, the increase in takeover attempts in recent years has resulted in a preoccupation on the part of both
boards and managements with seeking ways to avoid attack or to
prepare a defense. These efforts are both time-consuming and
expensive, and while they may be necessary, they are certainly
not productive.

One of the difficulties in takeover situations is that the board,
as the representative of the shareowners, may have somewhat
different interests and obligations than the management. In most
unfriendly takeovers that are successful, the senior management
of the target company becomes unemployed. A common accu-
sation, therefore, is that in resisting a takeover management is
simply trying to entrench itself, even though the deal, if it went
through, would result in a handsome gain for the shareowners.
Directors in these situations must exercise great care in making
certain that their decisions are in fact in the shareowners' inter-

ests. But this is not always easy to determine. There are difficult questions of valuation. What is the intrinsic value of the corporation? What is the real value of the "junk bonds" being offered to the shareowners? Also, what consideration, if any, should the directors give to the interests of other parties, such as employees and communities and customers, who could be affected by a change in ownership and a possible breakup of the company? Obviously, these are complex issues for the board to deal with.

Directors encounter special problems when the company's management attempts to acquire control through a leveraged buyout. In these situations, management typically will attempt to use unconventional financing—junk bonds, borrowing, and very little equity—to buy out the shareowners. Clearly, management and the outside directors are on the opposite sides of the table in these transactions. The outside directors must act completely independently of management, they must have their own legal and investment banking counsel, and they must make certain that whatever transaction is ultimately consummated is fully justified and can be defended on its merits.

In a hostile takeover attempt, a board's situation is further complicated by the fact that it is traversing a veritable legal minefield. Takeovers inevitably give rise to law suits, and recent court decisions bear importantly on the legal responsibilities and liabilities of directors. The harsh fact is that directors' potential liabilities are immense. In fact, many insurance companies which underwrite directors' and officers' insurance are now excluding hostile takeover situations from coverage under their liability policies. This is not the place (nor are we the ones) to discuss the legal issues involved in takeovers. But directors must know that they have exceedingly important legal obligations which require that they have competent expert advice when they are involved in takeover attempts.

In practice, when a hostile takeover is initiated the company's lawyers, investment bankers, accountants, and other advisors, together with the board and management, all become involved in a hectic struggle that can last for several weeks or months. It becomes a 24-hour-a-day, 7-day-a-week effort. Nearly everything else stops as there is intense preoccupation on survival—or on striking the best possible deal. When the episode is over, everyone involved will know they have experienced a crisis.

There are those who maintain that corporate takeovers are constructive. They root out inefficient and entrenched management. Economically nonviable business entities are shut down and capital is redeployed into more productive endeavors. And the shareowners benefit from the increased value of their shares. We do not agree with this position. Too many financial entrepreneurs have engaged in takeovers (or threatened takeovers) simply with short-term profiteering in mind. We would suggest that Mr. Icahn's acquisition of control of TWA in 1985 was a case in point. And even when takeovers are unsuccessful, the target company is often left in a severely weakened position as a result of its defensive tactics. Although Union Carbide succeeded in fending off a threat from GAF in early 1986, it did so at the expense of repurchasing 55 percent of its own stock, adding considerable debt, and agreeing to sell its consumer products division. It ended up a different and weaker company. Many other examples could be cited to demonstrate that hostile takeovers are often neither constructive nor in the public interest.

No matter how one may feel about this takeover trend, however, one thing is certain. It is a reality in today's business world and directors must be prepared to deal with the possibility that their company might be—or become—a target.

Defensive Tactics

What, if anything, can a board do to prepare for, or help to prevent, an unfriendly takeover? One precaution is to hire a law firm that specializes in counseling companies on tactics designed to minimize the chances of a raid. This firm will also work with the company in the event of a takeover attempt. Since these are events that deeply involve the board, some companies arrange for the law firm to meet informally with the board every year or so for an update on takeover activities. These meetings usually include a review of current takeover tactics, changes in the relevant laws and regulations, recommendations on measures designed to protect the company and appropriate responses if a takeover is attempted. These sessions provide directors with an opportunity, in a noncrisis atmosphere, to understand more clearly their legal options and obligations.

The company's investment banker is also often brought into these discussions. Valuation questions almost always arise and directors must have their expert advice. It is therefore advisable for the company's investment banker to be current on the company's situation and its plans. Moreover, an investment banker experienced in takeover situations can be helpful in devising tactics in the heat of a takeover battle. So both the company's legal counsel and its investment bank should be briefed and ready in the event they are needed.

On the advice of legal counsel, many firms have adopted so-called shark-repellent measures designed to discourage would-be aggressors. These include such measures as staggered board terms, super majority/fair price provisions, shareowners' rights plans, and other tactics limited only by the ingenuity of the lawyers. In some instances these maneuvers are warranted, but their effectiveness is unclear. Moreover, they have a subtle, hidden cost. Making it difficult to unseat management interferes with, and weakens, the process of corporate governance. In considering shark repellents, a board should recognize that in an effort to protect the company, it may be creating a situation in which the legitimate rights of the shareowners and other interested parties can be frustrated.

An example of shark repellent measures which caused unwarranted restrictions on shareowners' rights were the proposals in Commodore International's 1984 proxy statement. One proposal asked the shareowners to give the chairman (who owned 19.5 percent of the shares) an absolute veto over any merger attempted by an aggressor holding at least 24 percent of Commodore's shares. Another proposal sought to prohibit a shareowner holding 10 percent, or more of the company's stock from voting on a merger he had proposed. Recommending to shareowners that they approve such proposals is tantamount to asking that they forfeit their legitimate rights. In this situation it is natural to ask whether the Commodore board was seeking to protect the shareowners or to entrench management. Many institutional investors have adopted policies of voting against some measures designed to prevent takeovers. If a significant proportion of a company's ownership is in the hands of institutions it would be wise to check their policy on specific defensive measures before asking for shareowner approval. Don't risk suffering a defeat by the shareowners.

In setting up defenses, a device that has become increasingly common is the so-called golden parachute, which is designed to provide employment protection for senior management in the event of a takeover. The purported rationale is to protect your senior managers so they will seek the best possible deal for the shareowners, even though the consequences may be their own unemployment. We believe that some protection is warranted for the few top officers who would be vitally involved in critical negotiations on behalf of the shareowners. This small handful of executives should not have their attentions diverted by concern with their personal employment problems at such a stressful time. There is, however, no justification for protecting dozens of executives who *might* lose their jobs, but who do not play a significant role in the takeover negotiations. Moreover, an executive should not benefit from a golden parachute unless his employment is actually terminated. Merely consummating a takeover should not activate parachute payments.

Golden parachutes have been misused and in the past many corporate executives have received windfall payments that were totally unjustified. As a consequence, in 1984 the Congress stepped in with legislation which effectively limited golden parachute payments to amounts not exceeding three years' compensation in the event of an unfriendly takeover. Although this may be a reasonable restriction, it is regrettable that it had to be imposed by the government. One consequence of this legislation has been that golden parachutes have been legitimized by the government, so many more corporations are adopting them than was heretofore the case.

We believe that boards should anticipate the golden parachute issue before it arises. Don't wait until a takeover has been initiated to address it. One board, for example, granted golden parachutes to senior managers after a takeover attempt was underway. The company received considerable adverse publicity, which was embarrassing. More important, however, executives below the senior management level were extremely unhappy. Their reaction was: "Well, the top guys took care of themselves and left us out in the cold. Obviously, they could care less about us." This created an awkward problem for the very people it was designed to help.

Preparation

It was noted earlier that the board should be kept informed on issues involving takeovers. It is also important that management be organized in advance to deal with the emergency. There should be an up-to-date "game plan" with management people knowing their assignments. Organization also means choosing and briefing the law firm, investment banker, the proxy solicitor, the accountants, and perhaps others to assist and advise the company. Making these arrangements after the battle is joined is a waste of valuable time.

In the final analysis, it is the board itself that plays the key role in dealing with a takeover attempt. As we stated earlier, this type of crisis comes close to being the ultimate test of a board's capability and durability.

OTHER CRISES

Replacing the CEO and dealing with unfriendly takeover attempts are obviously not the only crises that confront boards. There are many others. Examples include the liquidity crisis of

the Continental Illinois Bank in 1984, the Bank of Boston's problems in 1985 involving unreported cash transactions, Lockheed's
problem with illegal payments in the 1970s, and Baldwin-
United's financial problems in 1983. Every week the *Wall Street
Journal* carries reports of companies going into bankruptcy or
into Chapter 11, companies being forced to merge because of
financial problems, companies suffering from major defalca-
tions, companies with serious product problems, and so on.

CONCLUSION

The reality of board membership is that from time to time a company will experience a crisis. It will probably be unexpected, and
it probably will be unpleasant. Nevertheless, the board should be
prepared to deal with the issues, no matter what their form or
severity. This is their obligation.

Whatever the nature of the crisis, it is usually the outside board
members who bear the brunt of the responsibility. The successful
resolution of these problems depends on the board's ability to
achieve consensus during a time of great pressure and to act
wisely and in the company's long-term interests. On these occasions board members are called on to devote far more time
than is convenient, and they must often deal with unpleasant situations. Successful handling of crises, however, is the essence
of board membership. The effective director does not shirk these
important responsibilities.

CASE
Capco Company—The Critically Ill Chairman

John McVay (age 58), chairman and CEO of Capco, was advised,
after a routine annual physical, that he had a serious health problem requiring immediate radical surgery. He would, at best, be

absent from the company for four to six months, and at worst he would never be able to return to work.

McVay immediately advised his board and suggested that any one of the three senior managers who were already on the board was qualified to be acting CEO during his absence. The board, meeting in executive session, selected one to be acting CEO, and he also acted as temporary chair at board meetings.

McVay's surgery was only partially successful and, in spite of extensive treatment, the outlook for his recovery was unclear. Nevertheless, eight months after the operation, although still seriously ill, he was convinced that he would ultimately recover and return to the company. Medical advice was guarded. The physicians would not make a specific prognosis and said that recovery was always possible. Others who were close to the situation, including several board members, were not optimistic about the prospects for the chairman's recovery, much less his return to work.

Despite the desire of every member of senior management to cooperate and "make do" during this interim period, it became clear that the organization was suffering because of the temporary leadership. The acting CEO was understandably reluctant to push ahead on major new projects or to make significant organizational changes. Moreover, the organization appeared to be waiting to see what would happen to McVay and whether the board would make a move. Decision making was stalled.

The outside board members met several times by themselves during this period. They all had a high regard for McVay's well-being, and were reluctant to take any step that might upset him. During these private and unofficial meetings, usually at dinner the night before the board meeting, one of the senior directors gradually emerged as the informal leader. At these meetings he urged anyone having pertinent information about the status of the chairman's health, or conditions within the company, to contribute his information and views. It was understandably difficult to obtain objective information on these subjects from management people, who were concerned both about McVay's health and the unsettled situation within the company. The other high-priority topic at these private meetings was the question of who the most suitable permanent successor would be if it became necessary to select one.

Finally, nearly nine months after McVay's operation, with his health continuing to deteriorate slowly and with ominous rumblings from within the organization, the outside board members decided that it was time to take action. By then they had decided that the acting CEO should become the new chairman and CEO. They invited him to an informal meeting and told him of their decision so that he could make appropriate plans. The senior director who had become the informal leader, and two other directors, took on the difficult task of visiting McVay and breaking the news to him. Immediately thereafter a short formal board meeting was held and announcements were released to the organization and the press that McVay had resigned and that the board had elected a new chairman and CEO.

Our Comment on Capco Company

It is significant to note that the most important work of the board was done outside the board's formal procedural framework. There was clearly a need for the outside board members to meet alone and to have private, informal discussions on the important issues with which they were dealing. This could hardly be done in the environment of the formal board meeting. Also, since the acting board chairman and CEO was an insider, the outside board members had to develop their own informal leadership. This is almost always true when a board is involved in selecting a CEO during a crisis situation, because in the large majority of cases the CEO is also the chairman of the board. The board's normal pattern of conducting its business is not appropriate in a crisis.

It is also noteworthy that in the midst of a crisis situation a director's time commitments significantly increase. No one else can do the job of selecting a new CEO, and a director must somehow find the time to participate with fellow outside directors to accomplish this assignment.

CASE
Telemix Company—When Is Action Necessary?

"Only when the company's results deteriorate almost to a fatal point," writes Harvard Professor Myles Mace, "does the board step in and face the unpleasant task of asking the president to resign."[1]

Looking back over the history of Telemix Company, John Talbott, a director from the beginning, wondered whether this description applied to its board. He also wondered whether the need for action should reasonably have been foreseen earlier.

Telemix Company was founded in 1956 by Ralph Belton. Its business was telecommunications and related aspects of high technology. From the start, the company was profitable, with its early growth coming mostly from acquisitions. However, in 1960 Belton became ill and was no longer able to work. A loss was incurred in that year.

In mid-1961, Belton was replaced by Charles E. Ongone, who had originally been hired as a consultant by Irving Abramson, a director, to "keep an eye on things" during Belton's illness. Ongone continued as chairman and CEO throughout the period covered by this case.

By 1963 the company had become profitable again. In 1966 its stock was listed on the New York Stock Exchange, and in August of that year it traded at a high of $350 a share (compared with its 1956 issue price of $0.50 per share). The stock was frequently referred to as "the darling of Wall Street." 1966 turned out to be the high point for both its share price and its earnings.

---

[1]Myles L. Mace, *Directors: Myth and Reality*, Boston: Division of Research, Harvard Business School (1971), p. 41.

Earnings began to decline after that, in part because of the loss of military contracts. The company had depended heavily on military work, and this work declined with the winding down of the Vietnam war. Telemix attempted to offset this loss by expanding its business in two directions. First, it became a multinational company by acquiring major distribution outlets in western Europe. Second, it developed proprietary commercial products.

From 1966 on, earnings per share were volatile: 1966, $4.04; 1967, $1.26; 1968, $3.10; 1969, $2.03; 1970, $2.15; and 1971, $2.75.

The Board.   As of the beginning of 1972, the board consisted of the following directors:

Charles E. Ongone, chairman and CEO.

John Talbott, partner in the brokerage firm that had arranged the original stock offering.

Three representatives of venture capital firms that had provided most of the original financing.

John Thornton, a university scientist who had been a consultant to the company since 1960.

Joseph Hanson, a former executive vice president of the company, and a board member since 1961.

Samuel Lefton, an early key member of the company's technical group, who became a director in 1966.

David Rector, a management consultant, who came to the attention of management in 1965 in the course of a consulting project, and who joined the board in 1966.

Walter Mall, founder of a company that Telemix acquired in 1966, and who became a board member in that year.

Lawrence Latham, a personal friend of Ongone's, who joined the board in 1970.

Sidney Ongone, brother of the CEO and a well-respected international lawyer, who joined the board in 1971.

Robert Smith, vice president of finance, and board member since 1971.

Latham, Sidney Ongone, and Smith replaced board members who had retired.

Initial Expressions of Concern. Joseph Hanson, executive vice president, became dissatisfied with Ongone's management ability in 1967. He discussed the matter informally with a few of the directors, including John Talbott, but was told that as long as there were earnings, there was no reason for the directors to intervene. Hanson resigned as executive vice president of Telemix in 1970, but retained his board membership. He was not popular with other board members.

Walter Mall became dissatisfied with Ongone's management in 1968. He resigned from his own position as president of the division he had formerly owned, but stayed on as a director. He had become wealthy as a result of the acquisition, and there was some feeling on the part of other board members that his resignation was an act of disloyalty.

By 1969 Mall had become so disturbed by the increase in overhead, especially research/development, that he discussed the matter informally with three other board members. Although each expressed some concern, none was willing to rock the boat. In late 1971 and again in early 1972, Mall called a meeting—after regular board meetings—to discuss the situation. The reaction was cold disapproval of his actions. In subsequent interviews, directors expressed their dislike for Mall. He was aware of this, and he said, "I am like the bastard at the company picnic that everyone wished wasn't there."

John Thornton began to question Ongone's decisions in the late 1960s, at first privately with friends on the board, including Talbott, and then openly at board meetings. Although he was a highly regarded scientist, Thornton's views were also disregarded. He was told privately by one outside director that "it was the norm of the Telemix board to vote unanimously in favor of

the CEO's recommendations." In 1971 Ongone proposed a new
retirement policy which was passed by the board. Since Thornton was four years beyond the mandatory age limit established
in that policy, his retirement was scheduled for August 1972.

In 1970 Ongone decided to introduce a product whose development was the responsibility of Lefton. Lefton felt strongly that
the product was not ready for market, and said so to Ongone and
to one of his fellow directors. He was overruled, and one director
advised Lefton to make his peace or leave.

Developments in Early 1972. In the January 1972 annual
meeting, Ongone publicly announced that he expected 1972
earnings (i.e., the year ending September 30, 1972) to show improvement over 1971, with the greatest gains coming in the fourth
quarter. Third-quarter earnings, released on July 4, were down
14 cents from those of a year before but in the report to shareholders Ongone repeated his expectation that fourth-quarter
earnings would be especially good. By then, the stock that had
traded at $350 in 1966 was selling for less than $50 a share. This
decline reflected Wall Street's disenchantment with the company's earnings estimates, which frequently turned out to be overly
optimistic.

In July 1972 Telemix borrowed $25 million from five insurance
companies. John Talbott's firm arranged the private placements.

Events of Fall 1972. The board meeting of August 1972 was
routine. The primary focus was on plans for new products, as
presented by division managers. The general impression of the
majority of the directors was that all was well.

On September 10, a financial journal announced that Telemix
would report a fourth-quarter operating loss and sharply lower
earnings for fiscal 1972, even though sales were expected to increase to $400 million, from $360 million in 1971.

On September 16, a special meeting of the executive committee was called. Management members present included Charles

Ongone; Smith, a director and financial vice president; and Stewart Jones, another vice president. Smith and Jones admitted that they had been concerned for some time, believing that there was too much emphasis on research/development projects and not enough on current operations. It also became apparent that management had known of the unfavorable prospects for several months.

Ongone, however, maintained that the situation was not as bad as it seemed. One director later said "I don't think he was consciously lying to us. But he had a way of hoping that things would get better."

The executive committee decided that research/development projects should be drastically reduced. They also gave Smith and Jones new responsibilities so that in effect they would be working with but not for the CEO.

Events in Fiscal 1973. On October 3, 1972, the four senior outside directors who had been involved in the founding of Telemix got together for lunch. They shared concern, but did not decide to act on it.

The board's dissatisfaction continued to increase. Consequently, they paid closer attention to monthly results. In addition, the board specifically directed the CEO not to make public statements of earnings estimates.

On January 19, 1973, the finance and audit committee held a regular meeting. Two days earlier Telemix had reported a modest first-quarter loss. By invitation, most of the directors were present. They were generally critical of management. On February 15, a combined meeting of the finance and audit committee and the executive committee was held. It was chaired by Hanson, not Ongone.

At the annual meeting of shareowners in February 1973, Ongone admitted that mistakes had been made in 1972 but said that he was optimistic about 1973. To some directors, his remarks seemed like an earnings forecast that the board had specifically prohibited him from making.

Conditions continued to deteriorate. Planned reductions in overhead were not achieved. Deadlines for projects were not met. Actual results for the second quarter were below budget. Three key members of management left. According to several directors, they had been squeezed out by Ongone.

Gradually, a consensus formed that was expressed by one director as follows:

It all culminated in a general feeling that Charles was one hell of a gentleman, one incredible character, a guy with a lot of vision, a guy with a lot of qualities of leadership, but a guy who was being overtaken on the bottom line by events that were occurring because of inadequate control of details.

Early in May, John Talbott invited the outside directors to a meeting in his office. Ongone knew of the meeting, asked to attend, but was not permitted to do so. Ongone thereupon asked Hanson to tell the directors that he planned to relinquish the role of CEO, but to remain as chairman. Accordingly, he suggested that the board arrange as soon as possible to bring into the company, or to promote from within, a new president and CEO. At the meeting, held on May 13, Ongone's proposal was discussed and quickly accepted. A search committee of the board was formed and began by hiring a search firm. Three members of the current management were suggested as potential candidates: Jones, Smith, and Robert Polar, who recently had been hired as director of marketing.

On July 21, 1973, third-quarter earnings were released; there was a net loss of 66 cents, compared with income of 70 cents a year earlier. Friends, investment houses, and others were pressuring board members to take action.

On October 9, 1973, Rex T. Gillette, senior vice president of marketing for one of Telemix's large competitors, was elected president and chief executive officer of Telemix Company, and Ongone was elected chairman.

Telemix reported an 82 cent loss in 1973, breakeven performance in 1974, and appeared to be on the way to satisfactory profits in 1975.

Our Comment on Telemix Company

In looking back, it seems clear that the board should have acted sooner than it did. The signs of poor management that existed in 1966 became obvious by 1972. Yet the new CEO was not selected until October 1973. The question is whether such a conclusion is based solely on hindsight. Should John Talbott, an original director, reasonably have been expected to act sooner?

There were powerful forces and assumptions inhibiting action, some of them related to the making of any unpleasant decision, and others peculiar to the removal of a CEO:

- The board had selected the CEO; to oust him would be an implicit admission that they had made a poor decision.
- A director who proposed removal might expect to be asked, Could you have done any better than he did? What would you have done differently? (even though these questions are not necessarily relevant).
- Several board members had family and professional ties to the CEO. If a director had initiated action, he might not have been able to obtain a majority vote. If he couldn't, the result would have been a divided board, incapable of accomplishing anything constructive.
- A related point: The CEO was a personal friend; he was particularly close to certain directors, who felt that it was wrong to abuse this friendship.
- Critics of the CEO had questionable motives: sour grapes, unfounded disagreements with his policies, desire to get his job.
- Ousting the CEO would require a search for a new one. Such

a search is difficult and time-consuming, and there is no assurance that a better CEO would be found.

- The company's difficulties stemmed from the decline in military contracts. Perhaps no one could restore it to its former profitability. The CEO might be doing an acceptable job in keeping the company alive under these circumstances. With better guidance as to research/development programs, the CEO should be given a chance to straighten things out.
- The CEO has served the company well; his competence has been proven. The directors should stick by him in adversity.

Despite these understandable arguments, we believe that the Telemix board made three mistakes: (1) It did not reach a decision soon enough. (2) Having reached a decision, it did not act promptly or decisively enough. (3) It had not made provisions for a successor.

In the late 1960s, there were indications of trouble. The executive vice president resigned (but retained his directorship). Mall, a director, division head, and founder of a successful company, informally expressed his dissatisfaction. Thornton, a respected scientist and member of the board since 1960, had qualms. Any one of these events should, by itself, have caused the board to investigate the situation; the allegations should have been thoroughly discussed with Ongone, and his responses appraised.

By September 1972, the CEO's reports were unreliable, and the board knew that they were unreliable; this alone is enough to warrant a lack of confidence and to justify a discussion. In what was an obvious move to get rid of a critic, the CEO initiated a new retirement policy that ousted the director who had been critical. In addition, three officers of the company quit.

In the face of this compelling evidence, all that the directors could bring themselves to do was to appoint two officers to work with but not for the CEO. This was a measure guaranteed not to succeed. In fact, when the board made this decision, it relieved Ongone of practically all responsibility for results. The decision muddied the leadership issue at the very time when clear lines of authority and responsibility were needed. It also prevented management from taking the strong and decisive steps needed to deal with the company's rapid deterioration.

Evidently, the directors could not overcome the norms of board behavior. (Don't rock the boat; support your CEO.) They were willing to reduce the CEO's freedom to act, but no more. Not until May 1973, eight months later, did they take the decisive step, and even then they seemed just to follow the CEO's lead. In our view, they should have initiated action to deal with the leadership issue in 1972. We realize that this is much easier said than done. However, in our opinion the board, in this case, clearly and simply failed to do its job.

Finally, the board had not identified a successor for the CEO. We noted in Chapter 2 that a key obligation of the board is to groom a suitable successor. In this case, the three management candidates were inadequate, and the board was forced to look outside for a replacement. While going outside is occasionally necessary, it is far more desirable to have an insider groomed to take over. There is no evidence that the board had paid the slightest attention to this issue until it became a pressing problem.

As we said earlier, with hindsight it is easy to be critical. However, we suggest that the Telemix board never did get its act together. It seemed incapable of working effectively within itself. Several directors appeared to have been alienated from others. There were several friends and relatives on the board, and they could hardly be expected to be objective. And there appears not to have been any leadership pattern among the outside board members. At one time the four senior outside board members met together. At another time the executive committee met with the audit and finance committee. Finally, Talbott took the initiative and called a meeting of the outside directors. Apparently this board never developed the sense of common purpose or rapport that any group needs in order to work effectively together. That is a shortcoming that may not be a problem in good times, but that is critical during a crisis. The Telemix board's failure to develop this quality or capability clearly contributed to its inability to function effectively when the crisis occurred.

In her 1984 book, *The March of Folly,* the Pulitzer prize-winning historian Barbara Tuchman demonstrates how throughout history, and especially during the Vietnam war, decision makers were unwilling to change existing policies, even though the need for change was evident. Perhaps this "folly" is inherent in human nature. Perhaps, however, recognition that this tendency exists will cause directors to counter it and to act more quickly than they currently do.

One seasoned board member who read this case observed that, given the composition of the Telemix board, it was expecting too much for it to deal promptly and decisively with Ongone. He pointed out that there was no one on the board with broad or significant corporate experience. Moreover, Ongone had arranged for one of his detractors to be retired and had loaded several friends and relatives on the board, together with two of his own executives. It was certainly not a board of independently minded executives experienced in dealing with tough corporate issues. It was a weak board, and this is probably just the way Ongone wanted it. Moreover, there is no evidence that anyone other than Ongone was involved in the selection of directors, which would ensure continuation of an inept board. This illustrates how important it is to give careful consideration to the composition of the board and how essential it is for the board to actively participate in the process of selecting new members. The next chapter on the nominating committee deals with this subject.

5
The Nominating Committee

A successful organization, whether it is a baseball team, a sales force, or a board of directors, consists of people who are well qualified to do their jobs. In this chapter we examine the characteristics of people and the combinations of people with various backgrounds that are necessary to comprise an effective board. We also address the process of finding, selecting, and attracting good board members. Our focus is on the role of the nominating committee, the means by which many boards participate in the process of deciding on board composition.

SIZE

As we indicated in Chapter 1, an effective board has between ten and 18 members. A board with fewer than ten has little room for including the variety of experienced people who can make useful contributions to board matters. At the other extreme, boards of 20 to 30 people are likely to be less than optimally effective. Large boards make it difficult for everyone to participate to the degree that they wish to, or should. As a result, much of the board's work must be done in committees, with only limited opportunity for discussion by the full board.

A board of up to 18 members allows adequate opportunity for active participation by members who have different backgrounds and experience. Interaction among directors determines the quality of a board's contribution, and the moderate-size board best provides opportunities for such interaction.

INSIDERS VERSUS OUTSIDERS

In recent years it has become a widely accepted practice for a majority of board members to be outsiders; that is, they are not employees of the corporation. A director who is also a corporate executive reporting to the chairman can hardly be expected to act independently of, or contrary to, the chairman's wishes. To do so might well put his career in jeopardy. A good board, therefore, consists largely of outsiders for whom there is no such conflict.

While the concept of the outside board is generally accepted, there are a number of excellent companies, such as Dow Chemical, and Deere and Company, that have a majority of insiders on their boards. Their proponents point out that having a majority of outsiders does not necessarily assure a good board. They believe that the advantage of having experienced company executives making board decisions is more important than having a majority of outsiders on the board who usually have limited knowledge of the company's business. While we favor the outside board, we do acknowledge that outsiders are not always strong contributors. However, we believe that the best way to deal with this problem is to have more effective outsiders, not to move toward an inside board.

There are, however, important reasons for having some insiders on the board. The chairman's probable successor should be a board member and should have full knowledge of, and be a participant in, the board's activities. If a successor has not been selected, the principal candidates are often elected to the board. This provides an opportunity for outside board members to become acquainted with them and to assess their capabilities. Moreover, since these potential candidates are senior officers who are intimately acquainted with corporate operations, they can make useful contributions to the board's discussions. Board membership can help these candidates develop by allowing them to gain experience in another dimension of corporate activity and leadership.

One caution. An inside board member gains a special status within the company. The board position is prestigious, meaningful to the person, to the organization, and to the outside world. Consequently, an insider should not be elected to the board unless it is understood that he will remain on the board only as long as his performance in both excecutive and directorship roles is satisfactory. Normally, that board membership terminates when the executive retires or leaves the company, and this expectation should be made clear upon his election to the board.

QUALIFICATIONS

The literature on boards contains long lists of qualifications for directors, including: integrity, experience, intelligence, judgment, and the like. These are familiar attributes of outstanding people, and we will not reiterate the obvious. There are, however, other important dimensions to a board's composition.

One is that the membership of a good board will include persons qualified to deal with various issues faced by the individual company. For example, a regional bank would have different board requirements from those of a large, technically oriented company whose principal customer is the U.S. Department of Defense. As another example, Federated Department Stores should have a different board from General Motors. This is not to say that a General Motors director would not be qualified to serve on Federated's board. It simply means that the mix of the board members' backgrounds, experience, and other qualifications should be different. And this mix should reflect the needs of the individual corporation.

The other dimension of a good board is a balanced membership—balance of occupation, experience, age, gender, race, geographical representation, and so on. In general, it is beneficial to have people from several different industries on the board. They can bring important insights to board meetings, based on their varied experiences. It is also helpful to have someone on the board with experience in the public sector, as this person contributes a perspective frequently missed by the business person. An academic can add still another perspective. Our point is that a board consisting of persons with varied backgrounds can engage in discussions with a richness and breadth that inevitably lead to better decision making. A board with diverse membership will also have an extensive network of contacts throughout industry, government, and the professions, that can be useful to the company in many ways.

Bankers and Counsel

A question frequently arises as to whether the company's attorney, or commercial or investment banker, should be a member of the board. The argument against this is that there may be conflicts between their duties as a director and their principal occupation or profession. For example, a CEO may feel obliged to use the firm of the invstment banker who is on his board, rather than to seek competitive proposals, or he may be reluctant to question the banker's charges. Many such potential problems and conflicts can arise.

On the other hand, there are many situations in which the banker or investment banker can provide advice of inestimable value to the company. Small companies that were originally financed by venture capitalists (who in most instances are actually specialized investment bankers) have boards that typically include representatives of the financing firm or firms. These board members often provide the experienced guidance and business judgment that is crucial to the success of a growing company. The same is true of the company's outside attorney or commercial bank. To generalize, therefore, that attorneys and commercial and investment bankers should *never* be board members would, in our opinion, be wrong.

In large publicly held companies, it is probably preferable that investment and commercial banking services, as well as legal services, be obtained separately from, and independent of, board membership. This distinction eliminates any possibility of conflict or abuse of privilege. We would not want to see those who provide these services, however, automatically barred from serving on boards. With appropriate sensitivity to potential conflict and with full disclosure, these people can be effective directors.

Age

A company with a mandatory retirement policy must keep in mind the retirement schedule when considering new directors. Having several directors of similar age (requiring them to retire within a short period of one another) can be disruptive to the board's continuity.

Gender and Race

For many good reasons, companies in the United States have been under considerable pressure to include more women and minorities on their boards of directors. In general, companies have been slow to respond. In some cases, this posture reflects an outmoded view of society. More commonly, boards have actively sought qualified women and minorities but have been unable to locate them. The pool of experienced, capable individuals is relatively small, and well-known members are already on as many boards as they can feasibly serve. Most corporations have wisely resisted "tokenism." Considering that board membership is likely to be indefinite, selection based upon ability and competence should not be compromised. As time goes on, more and more women and minorities will be qualified for board membership. Companies should tap this growing talent pool. Doing so will not only enhance the board's quality, but also will add other perspectives to the mix.

Women and minorities who are invited to join a board will sometimes feel that the invitation is merely a show of tokenism. Such individuals should be convinced to feel otherwise, for the invitation should reflect the board's belief that the person is in all respects qualified and welcome. The consequences of electing someone who is unqualified or who is likely to be disruptive are too serious to permit any other conclusion.

CEOs

Boards seeking new members understandably want to attract top people, people with proven experience, and people whose names will lend prestige to the organization. Thus, most boards have chairmen and CEOs from other corporations. Their experience with board and top-level corporate matters qualifies them to be helpful as outside directors. Robert Hatfield, former chairman of The Continental Group, Inc., has remarked, "With several CEOs on your board, you can't make a mistake. At least one of them will have lived through any new problem, challenge, or opportunity you face." While Hatfield's guarantee against mistakes is an overstatement, it is nevertheless clear that CEOs can be valuable directors.

Two other important types of candidates are senior executives likely to become CEOs of their companies and retired chairmen and CEOs. Depending on the desired qualifications for a new director (e.g., age, industry background, gender) these two pools can be helpful in achieving the desired balance on the board.

Major Shareowners

Two other categories of persons who qualify for board member-ship are individuals who are major shareowners, and directors who join a board representing the interests of a powerful group of shareowners. They often have an *a priori* right to be on the board. Indeed, in many instances they can simply vote themselves onto the board. However, once on the board they have an obligation to act in the interest of all shareowners, not simply themselves. Moreover, they have (at least legally) no more authority than any other board member. Each director has one vote, regardless of the number of shares he owns.

Practically speaking, however, it is hard for a director who owns a token number of shares not be be influenced by a director who owns, for example, 20 percent of the company. If a large shareowner director insists on throwing his weight around, he is likely to drive away the conscientious director who owns little stock but who is sensitive to his directorship obligations. Many businesses have failed to achieve their potential because a dominant shareowner has been unable or unwilling to subordinate his ego sufficiently so that the company can build a really effective board of directors.

THE SELECTION PROCESS

The board should have a defined and agreed-upon process for the selection of its members. Although legally the board is elected by the shareowners, as a practical matter boards are pretty much self-perpetuating bodies. The process of selecting board members is therefore of fundamental importance to the future of the corporation. Unfortunately, in many companies this process is loose and ill-defined. The chairman often dominates the decisions with respect to new board members, and the full board is effectively precluded from participating in the selection process. Myles L. Mace says,

Change initiated by directors is unlikely because the power and control of large, widely held corporations lies in the office of the CEO. Control

*of the proxy system enables the CEO to design the membership of the
board in any way he chooses.*

When this happens, the board is abrogating an important responsibility that it has to the shareowners and other constituents. The next generation of directors will determine the quality
of the company's future management. No board should leave this
solely to the CEO's discretion.

An important and constructive trend in the past decade has
been the more active use of the nominating committee in the
selection of board members. Ideally, this committee is composed
of several senior outside board members and the CEO. The chairman of the nominating committee should be one of the outside
board members, not the CEO. The committee's charter is typically to review candidates to be considered for nomination and
to make its recommendations to the full board.

This committee also considers the continuing eligibility of current board members—a delicate matter, since it is not easy to
vote against the renomination of a fellow board member. Consequently, nominating committees routinely recommend current
board members for renomination. While this practice is understandable, in some cases it is unfortunate. Too often, directors
who are clearly unable or unwilling to fully perform their duties
are retained because no one faces up to the problem. One experienced corporate director asks, "Why don't we have performance reviews for directors?" In fact, this director recently
surprised the chairman of a board that he was on by asking for
a performance review. How many directors would do this? If,
however, this became an accepted practice, the turnover among
directors would probably increase, and we would have better
boards. Unfortunately, this is not likely to happen soon, because
of the power of peer pressure. Nevertheless, we believe that
nominating committees should be increasingly sensitive to the
competence level of fellow directors when making their recommendations for director nominees.

The Sage Company case at the end of this chapter provides an
illustration of how a nominating committee functions.

DECIDING TO JOIN A BOARD

Joining a board should be an act of commitment, and the decision should be made thoughtfully. Usually, the first reaction to an invitation is to feel flattered, as it's nice to know that you are wanted. Often it is like being invited to join an exclusive club. But there is a great deal more involved. Commitment of time, travel, dealing with troublesome and disagreeable situations, possible conflicts and even potential personal liability are all embodied in board membership. Careful consideration is important.

If you are potentially interested, there are some obvious matters to be investigated. Would there be a conflict of interest? Can you spend the time required, and are the meeting dates compatible with your calendar of commitments? Then there are more subtle, but perhaps more important, considerations. Ernest C. Arbuckle, former dean of Stanford's Graduate School of Business, chairman of Wells Fargo Bank, and an experienced director, suggests asking: Why do you want me to be a director of your company? The answer should indicate whether you have been chosen as a result of a careful, deliberate process, or whether you were someone who just happened to come to mind. Do they want you just for your name, or are they seriously interested in what you can contribute? You should be comfortable with the reasons given for wanting you to join.

Then, of course, you will need to learn what you can about the company. Read some annual reports. Is the company sound and making progress, or is it declining and in trouble? Read the proxy statements. What is your assessment of the board members? Do you know any of them, and if so, are they people with whom you will feel comfortable sharing board responsibilities? If a majority are insiders, some special care is warranted. You might be uncomfortable with the idea of being on a board where the insiders would control the majority votes—irrespective of the view of the outside, independent directors.

Consideration should also be given to what you can realistically expect from joining a board. Will it be an experience from which you can learn and grow in your own career? Are the personal contacts constructive? Is the compensation appropriate? And, of course, you will need to obtain permission from your own board (assuming you are a CEO) or employer.

These are but a few of the considerations involved in deciding whether to join a board. Many board members have said yes to a flattering invitation only to regret their decision later, when they discovered unexpected problems or circumstances with which they were uncomfortable. We repeat our opening sentence: Joining a board should be an act of commitment, and the decision should be made thoughtfully.

RESIGNATION

Occasionally, directors resign. Sometimes the reason is purely personal—such as health. On other occasions a board member may consider resigning to avoid troublesome situations. In considering this action, the director should remember that he was elected by the shareowners and is expected to act in the company's interests. If a director has a real understanding of this obligation, he should resign only under the most extreme circumstances. In fact, the more difficult the company's situation becomes, the more important a director's role becomes.

Moreover, a director needs to be sensitive to the implications of resignation. The abrupt withdrawal of a director can carry a strong message to the investment community, banks, shareowners, customers, vendors, and employees. It can suggest serious problems within the company. This is not to say that a director should never resign; rather, he should be aware that doing so can create awkward problems for those left behind.

If, however, a director has sound reasons for being disturbed about the company's policies and has exhausted every reasonable avenue—with both the CEO and fellow directors—resigning may indeed be the proper thing to do. The issue, however, must be absolutely crucial to the company's survival, and the relative positions clearly drawn. The director must feel deeply that he is morally and professionally right.

An example, in our opinion, of justifiable resignation was in the case of the Bendix Corporation in 1982. Bill Agee, the Bendix chairman, initiated an unfriendly takeover effort against Martin Marietta Corporation. The matter was ultimately resolved in the takeover of Bendix by Allied Corporation, but not until after Bendix had acquired 70 percent of Martin Marietta. In the final phase of this unfortunate spectacle, four Bendix directors resigned. Although the individual directors involved have been appropriately discreet in their comments, it is widely surmised that Agee acted without consulting his board. Agee had presumably usurped the board's powers, and, as we have said before, no self-respecting, conscientious board member should be willing to be a rubber stamp. Under these circumstances, a responsible director cannot be criticized for resigning. Indeed, the board's only alternative would have been to replace Agee—but by then, for all practical purposes, the ball game was over.

Deciding not to stand for reelection is very different from deciding to resign. A board member must feel free either to stand for reelection or to decline to be on the slate of director nominees. There can be many valid reasons for declining, and if a director believes he should withdraw from further participation—for whatever reasons—the proper way to do it (except in the most extreme circumstances) is simply not to stand for reelection.

RETIREMENT

The composition of a board is obviously influenced by the company's retirement policy for directors. Some boards have no retirement policy. Others have strict policies, with retirement ages as low as 65. In recent years there has been a trend for boards to adopt compulsory-retirement plans, with the most common retirement age being 70.

Dealing with directors' retirements can be a sensitive issue. Most people (including ourselves) do not appreciate being reminded that they are getting old. Moreover, being asked to relinquish a directorship often signals the end of a long and perhaps illustrious career. Without a strict policy, a board is faced with offending an honored colleague or looking to a board of superannuated members. These, of course, are both undesirable alternatives. They can be avoided, at least in part, with an agreed-upon and consistently applied retirement policy.

PRE-RETIREMENT REVIEW OF BOARD SERVICE

In addition to retirement at a specified age, some companies have the policy of reviewing a director's status if that director substantially changes or reduces his or her level of business or professional activity for an extended period of time. The theory is that such a change in circumstances can result in a lessening of interest, a narrowing of perspective, an impairment of judgment, and general reduction of a director's effectiveness.

It is important that such a policy be known and understood by all directors and that a procedure for its implementation be outlined. One company has adopted the following procedure in the event that a board member has a changed or inactive status that continues for a period of three years:

Step 1. The CEO consults with the nominating committee.

Step 2. Following this consultation, there is a discussion between the CEO and the director.

Step 3. The CEO reviews results of the discussion with the nominating comittee.

Step 4. The nominating committee discusses the situation and recommends to the board what action, if any, is appropriate.

Step 5. In each individual case this procedure is repeated in subsequent years at the discretion of the CEO.

This company has also specified that the procedure be activated in the event that the special reason for which a person was placed on the board no longer pertains. An example would be if a person joined the board as a result of an acquisition in which he became a large stockholder—and then he disposed of the stock. The company's detailed policy provides a useful safeguard against retaining board members who no longer perform their duties effectively, irrespective of age.

CONCLUSION

The quality of the board is obviously determined by the people who comprise its membership. A good board has members who are qualified to deal with the issues of a particular company's business. What would be a good board for one company would not necessarily be good for another. Any good board, however, has individuals of diverse backgrounds who can bring experienced and fresh viewpoints to board discussions and decision making.

The board selection process is important since it determines the quality of the company's future board. Many boards have a nominating committee which is responsible for selecting candidates for board membership and recommending the slate of nominees to the full board. Membership of the nominating committee should include the CEO and several outside board members. It should, however, be chaired by an outside director—not the CEO.

CASE
Sage Company—Joining the Board

Lee Kern was a member of the board of the Sage Company and of its nominating committee. In early 1984 a question was raised at a meeting of this committee regarding the suitability of a new candidate. Kern was unsure as to what his position should be.

Sage had ten outside and two inside board members. (See Table 1). The insiders were the chairman–CEO, Earl Royse, and the president and chief operating officer, David Wendell. The outsiders were all persons of considerable prominence from business and other professions. It was regarded as a good board. Sage was considered to be one of the top six firms in its industry. Annual sales exceeded $2 billion. The company had six divisions located throughout the United States and twenty plants producing a wide variety of containers and packaging products.

The nominating committee consisted of four outside board members (including Kern) and Earle Royse. Jim Morrell, one of the outside board members and a former U.S. Government cabinet member, served as chairman. He opened the February 1984 meeting by noting that the committee needed to deal with two important matters.

The first item on the agenda was to consider and recommend to the full board the slate of directors to be included in the proxy statement for the annual shareowners meeting scheduled for early May. There were no vacancies on the board, and after a brief discussion, it was agreed that all the current board members be recommended for reelection.

The second item on the agenda concerned filling a vacancy that was scheduled to occur at the time of the 1985 annual meeting. At that time, a senior director would retire under the company's established age limit, and Royse was anxious to have a new director of suitable qualifications either on board or available to stand for election at the 1985 annual meeting. Since the board could legally increase or decrease its own membership, there would be no problem in adding a new board member sometime during the year.

In 1983, the nominating committee had begun the process of narrowing its candidate list down to two or, at the most, three, for more intensive screening. Royse's office maintained an active list of director candidates, and at each meeting of the nominating committee this list was updated. Names were both added and deleted, based upon the committee's deliberation. A week

Table 1
Sage Company:
Composition of Board of Directors

	Title or Occupation	Age	Years on Board
Inside Directors			
Earle Royse[a]	Chairman and CEO	57	8
David Wendell[a]	President and COO	49	4
Outside Directors			
Jim Morrell[a]	Investor—former cabinet officer	61	8
Lee Kern[a]	Retired—university president	67	6
Ralph Pica[a]	President and CEO, U.S. Energy Co.	59	5
A[a]	Retired—former owner of company acquired by Sage	64	12
B	Dean, leading engineering school	55	1
C	Chairman and CEO of an apparel manufacturing company	57	3
D	Investor and property developer	69	15
E	Attorney	52	6
F	Retired—president of a mining company	65	3
G	Investor—former owner of company acquired by Sage	62	14

[a] Member of Nominating Committee

before the February meeting, Royse had mailed to each committee member a current list of director candidates, which included considerable biographical and reference data. In 1983 Royse had initiated a discussion about the desirable qualifications of the next director. It was agreed, in light of the current composition of the board, that the new director ideally would be in his early to mid-fifties and should be the CEO of a successful and prominent manufacturing company. In late 1983 the committee considered all the candidates on the list and after some discussion narrowed the list to two, Carl Randall and Jeff Henley.

Kern was well acquainted with Carl Randall and thought he would make an ideal addition to the Sage board. Randall, age 50, was the president and CEO of the Supra Company which manufactured a line of high-technology products. Supra was frequently referred to as one of America's best-managed companies. Kern had known Randall for 15 years and considered him to be one of the two or three best executives in the country. He had been CEO of Supra for two years and was only on one board in addition to his own. It was surmised that he could take his pick whenever he wished to add to his board memberships.

Royse also knew Randall very well and in fact had for several years been—and still was—a member of Supra's board. It was Royse who had originally suggested Randall as a candidate for Sage's board.

The other candidate, Jeff Henley, was the CEO of an outstanding manufacturing firm. Henley was not well known to anyone on the committee, but his credentials were excellent. His company was the leading firm in its industry, and he had a splendid record as CEO. Moreover, the committee had several confidential reports about Henley from persons known to some committee members. In each instance he was reported to be "top notch" as a candidate for director. He was 52 years old.

Kern indicated that he favored Randall, and he commented on his outstanding qualities as both a businessman and a person. He added that if Sage didn't pursue Randall now, he probably would not be available later.

After further discussion, the committee chairman, Jim Morrell, raised a question that had not yet been considered. He noted that Royse was on the board of U.S. Energy Corp.—America's fifth largest oil and energy company—and that U.S. Energy's president and CEO, Ralph Pica, was also on the Sage board. In fact, he was a member of the nominating committee. Morrell's question to the committee was: Randall's qualifications aside, would it be wise to have two people on the Sage board, Pica and Randall, who were CEOs of companies on whose boards Royse was also a board member? Committee members voiced differing opinions. One view was that Randall's qualifications were sufficiently outstanding to override the fact that Royse was on his company's board. The other view was concern that having CEOs serving on each other's boards might be viewed by shareowners and the public as being a *club* where CEOs looked out for one another's interests. Also, while Randall was outstanding, Henley was also clearly very well qualified.

Kern was confident that both Royse and Randall would try to act with complete independence and integrity. The more he thought about it, however, the more concerned he became about appointing Randall. Quite apart from appearances and qualifications, was it wise to have two Sage directors, Pica and Randall, who were also CEOs of companies (U.S. Energy and Supra) on whose boards Royse served? Thus, while Kern still thought that Randall was the more attractive candidate, he wondered if his strong position was justified.

Throughout the committee's discussion, Royse indicated that he would be happy with either candidate.

Our Comment on Sage Company

The Sage Company case, in addition to posing a problem for Lee Kern, provides noteworthy illustrations of nominating committee practices.

The committee's first order of business was to consider the slate of directors for the next annual meeting. The board of directors is able to exercise appropriate control over the process by which board membership is determined through the activities of the nominating committee. Without this committee, the CEO would be in a position to dominate the selection of board members. In the Sage Company case there is no evidence of excess domination by Royse, the CEO. While the case does not specify the extent of the committee's discussion regarding the qualification of current directors, there was an organized forum established for the outside directors to participate in this process.

The process followed by the committee in the selection of a new board member also illustrates practices that are constructive. In the first place, the committee maintains and regularly updates a list of candidate directors. Earle Royse participates in this effort, and his office assists by maintaining the list, collecting biographical data, and so on. There is no evidence, however, that he dictates who should and should not be included on the list. Having such a candidate list is an excellent practice.

Second, when it came time to choose a new director, the criteria to be used by the committee had already been discussed. Royse had raised this issue well in advance so that the selection process could proceed in an orderly fashion. In this case the board had agreed that it was seeking a CEO of a leading manufacturing company in his early fifties. Obtaining agreement in advance on the desired characteristics for a new director is a constructive practice. Otherwise there is a tendency to select an *attractive* person without regard to the effect he might have on the board's balance.

Finally, it is significant that the committee discussed the new director issue a year in advance of the next retirement. A good candidate, after he is approached, will want to think carefully about the prospective commitment. This usually involves learning something about the company's business and who its directors are, considering possible conflicts of interest, looking at time commitments and schedules, among other matters. If the position looks interesting, the candidate should obtain his board's permission to assume this added obligation. All of this will normally take several months. If, during or at the end of this process, candidate number one decides he cannot accept the proffered directorship, it is important that there be time available to initiate discussions with candidate number two. Given this sequence of events, a year is certainly not too much lead time for seeking a qualified new director.

The primary issue in the Sage case concerns the appropriateness of CEOs serving on one another's boards. Certainly there are instances in which boards have become excessively inbred. Or at least there is the danger that critics will perceive this to be the case. The problem is aggravated in this case by the already-existing overlap, since Royse is on the board of U.S. Energy as well. Would two such overlapping board memberships be too much, even though Randall is highly qualified and Kern has utmost confidence in everyone's independence and integrity?

The resolution of Lee Kern's dilemma is not simple. However, there is an important principle involved. Irrespective of a person's qualifications, it is understandable that CEOs on each other's boards would have a natural tendency to support one another. This is not to imply that they would compromise their judgment on any important matter. In fact, we are convinced that in the vast majority of instances this would not be the case. Nevertheless, the circumstance is created where this could happen. It is not a healthy arrangement, and in general boards should avoid such overlappings of chairman and/or CEOs. We believe that in the Sage Company case it would be prudent not to select Randall, especially since the alternate candidate seems well qualified and is quite acceptable to Royse.

It is important—and should be comforting to the board—that Royse did not lobby for Randall. This indicates that Royse was not seeking to pack the Sage board with friends who might automatically support him. In addition, it is encouraging that Morrell, the chairman of the nominating committee, raised the issue of overlapping directorships, thereby displaying sensitivity to and understanding of the role of the committee in the director selection process.

CASE
Rushforth Company—When Do Directors Retire?

As of April 1984, the date of the Rushforth Company annual meeting, Bill McLean would reach the mandatory retirement age of 70 and would not be eligible for reelection as a director. Early in 1984, some of the directors questioned the soundness of the company's retirement policy.

The CEO, other members of senior management, and the members of the board were unanimously of the opinion that McLean was an extraordinarily effective director. He had more board seniority than any other director, and for many years he had been chairman of the compensation committee. Whenever he spoke at meetings, his advice was excellent. During his tenure he had found amicable resolutions to several disagreements among other directors. He worked closely with the CEO, and the CEO often sought his counsel informally.

Rushforth Company had been in existence for more than 75 years. Beginning in 1950, the management had embarked on a diversification and expansion program, and in 1970 the company entered the ranks of the Fortune 500. Its CEO, several other members of senior management, and several directors were members of, or related to, the family whose forebears started the company.

In 1977 the company fell on hard times. Its profits rapidly turned into large losses, it ran out of working capital, it failed to comply with certain covenants in its bonds, and the price of its stock dropped from 80 to about 15.

With the encouragement and support of the board, Bill McLean headed an ad hoc three-person committee to correct the situation. The committee arranged for the CEO to retire, received the resignation of several other senior managers, selected a division president as the new CEO, and arranged for the co-operation of the bondholders, all within the space of a few months. The new management turned the company around. It became profitable within a year, and profits increased steadily thereafter. The stock price reached 80 again by 1982, and continued to increase.

As part of the 1977 reorganization, the owners of three large blocks of stock, two of whom were over age 60, were added to the board. At that time, two other directors, members of the founding family, were in their 70s. In 1977 the board passed a resolution requiring directors to retire when they reached age 70; in most cases they would be elected honorary directors thereafter. (Honorary directors could attend board meetings, but were expected not to participate in the discussion and had no vote.)

As of 1984, two of the directors elected in 1977 and two family directors were honorary directors. Only one of them regularly came to board meetings. Another honorary director, unrelated to the family, was a prominent investment banker who had reached retirement age in 1983 and who did not like the idea of retiring; he did not attend meetings.

Bill McLean was in excellent health and as intelligent and articulate as ever. Five years earlier he had retired as CEO of a company that had a policy of mandatory retirement at age 65. He continued as director of two other Fortune 500 companies that did not have a mandatory age limit for directors. Although some of the directors kidded Bill about being caught up by the retirement rule that he was instrumental in establishing, Bill had never commented on his own situation. Several directors believed, however, that he would like to continue to participate in Rushforth affairs.

On one hand, the board wanted Bill to remain a member. On the other hand, some board members attributed the company's earlier difficulties to the presence of elderly board members. They did not want the company to have this problem again. They also knew that if an exception were made for Bill McLean, the investment banker and the other honorary directors who were large shareholders would feel that they had been discriminated against. All four were personal friends of most board members.

Our Comment on Rushforth Company

The Rushforth case illustrates at least three important aspects of the retirement issue.

First, there is evidence that at least some portion of the problems that resulted in the 1977 crisis were attributable to the board. At that time the board included a number of elderly members, several of whom were members of the family that had founded the company. Presumably they were reluctant to allow the board to take the decisive action needed to forestall serious difficulty.

It is not unusual for elderly directors, who may have longtime family and company allegiances, to have difficulty facing tough issues. This is especially true when, for example, the decision requires the removal of long-time executives. While these decisions can be difficult under any circumstances, they may become nearly impossible for a board of elderly family directors. Indeed, to subject elderly board members to this kind of pressure may be quite unfair. A retirement policy, consistently implemented, can help to avoid such unfortunate situations.

A second observation concerns the major contribution made by Bill McLean. He had obviously provided the leadership that was needed to remedy the company's problems. Among the several actions taken by the board in 1977 was adoption of the retirement policy—undoubtedly in response to the problems the company had experienced. Bill—and the board—wanted to minimize the chance of a recurrence.

The third observation concerns that policy itself. Now that Bill is approaching the mandatory retirement age, the policy is in question. The case illustrates a fact of life. People age quite differently, and Bill McLean at 70 happens to be vigorous and wise. There seems little doubt that he could continue as an effective director for some years to come. Other people, however, after retirement from their regular occupation at 65 become less active and involved, or develop interests that remove them from contact with the business world. In either case, such people soon become ineffective board members.

There obviously is no magic retirement age. No matter what age is established, it will be too high in some cases and too low in others. However, if a company is to have a retirement policy *some* age limit needs to be set and adhered to. If an exception is made for Bill McLean, others will feel that they have been discriminated against and the company might as well have no policy. When will Bill retire? Will he run out of steam at age 71, 72, . . . , ever? What happens when the next director becomes 70?

We are divided on this issue. One of us believes that if the company truly wants a retirement policy it must have the guts to implement the policy on a consistent basis, even though in the situation at hand it may be difficult or even seem unwise. It is better in the long run for the company to have a retirement policy and thereby to avoid the potential problems of superannuated directors than it is to make an exception to keep an unusual director, such as Bill McLean, on the board.

The other author takes the other view. He believes that some way should be found to keep Bill's talent available to the board, and if the only way of doing this is to change the retirement policy, for example, to 72, he would favor doing so.

As a retired director, Bill is eligible to become an honorary director. This is a distinction he clearly deserves and which the board should offer him. He would become the sixth honorary director. This raises a question as to how many honorary directors a company should retain; should a limit be put on the tenure of these directors? The company has established a precedent that may become awkward to change. Unfortunately, sometimes honorary directors tend to forget they are merely honorary. Moreover, it may be hard for them to give up the pleasure they derive from coming to board affairs. Therefore, with the very best of intentions on all sides, the honorary director position can become a problem, and it should not be initiated without careful consideration. Rather than have honorary directorships, many companies invite retired directors to special occasions and accord them appropriate recognition in this manner.

The Outcome

The chairman of the board, who was also CEO, did not want to lose McLean's services. After informal consultation with several board members, he proposed that McLean be retained as a consultant to him and to the compensation committee. He would be urged to attend board meetings as a nonvoting honorary director. The consulting arrangement was for one year and could be renewed annually. As a consultant, he would be asked to develop a new compensation plan to replace the current one that was to expire in two years. The board enthusiastically accepted this proposal, and it was so recorded in the minutes (although it did not require formal board approval).

The potential problem with this solution is that it might generate negative feedback from the current honorary directors, particularly those who own large blocks of stock. This problem did not develop, however, during the first year after McLean's official retirement.

Both of us agree that this solution was a good one.

6

The Compensation Committee

The board, in its governance role, determines compensation for the CEO and the other principal corporate officers. In practice, many boards delegate this function to a compensation committee. This committee, composed of outside board members, makes its recommendations to the full board for review and approval. This chapter explores the role of the compensation committee and the principal issues it must deal with. It is not an exposition on executive compensation policies.

CEO COMPENSATION

When the board sets the CEO's compensation, it is also establishing a compensation standard for managers throughout the company. Their compensation is integrally related to the CEO's, and this is therefore the single most important compensation decision the board must make.

In most instances this decision is not an easy one. A CEO is typically ambitious and competitive, and his report card is his compensation. Since his compensation and that of his peers are disclosed in proxy statements, he is able to see just where he stands in relation to others. Virtually every CEO would like to stand higher on that list. Thus, the compensation committee is dealing with a highly sensitive issue affecting the corporation's most important person.

If the CEO's compensation is significantly higher than that of competing organizations, management compensation costs add a burden to the company's cost structure. In addition, the compensation of top corporate executives has become an issue of public concern. Sensational news stories about top business executives' income, while often misleading and sometimes downright wrong, can stir up emotions antagonistic to the company or the business community.

Arjay Miller, retired dean of Stanford's Graduate School of Business and former president of Ford Motor Company, says that the best bargain a board can get for the shareowners is to pay a high salary for a really superior CEO. We agree with his observation, but at the same time we feel that a board must be sensitive to the shareowners, labor unions, employees, and the public, with respect to what they feel is appropriate compensation.

In the midst of these conflicting pressures, the compensation committee must make its decisions. In doing so, there are three principal guidelines to keep in mind. The CEO's compensation should:

- Be related to performance.
- Be competitive.
- Provide motivation.

Performance

The CEO's compensation must be related to his performance. Superior performance should be rewarded with high compensation, while poor performance, if not warranting dismissal, should at least result in minimal compensation. There is justification to the claim that in some companies top-executive compensation just keeps going up and up, without regard to performance. The problem is complex. Presumably, the CEO should be rewarded for increasing the value of the shareowner's wealth over the long term. Although this is a splendid generalization, the criterion is hard to measure, especially on a year-to-year basis. Compensation committees, therefore, are forced to rely largely on subjective judgments and some long-term arrangements, such as stock options or performance share plans, which hopefully, albeit imperfectly, relate compensation to performance.

The crux of the problem is: What kind of performance or set of accomplishments does the board expect and how are they to be measured? Unfortunately, many compensation committees fail to address this problem systematically. They have no useful or agreed-upon standards against which the CEO's performance is measured. Should they judge it by the increase or decrease in earnings per share? By whether the company maintained the current level of earnings while investing in a new generation of products that will ensure future growth? By changes in the debt/equity ratio? By whether the CEO has engineered an acquisition or a divestiture? Or by whether he has brought in a competent outside executive as a potential successor? The list can be endless. The point is that unless there is an understanding with the CEO as to where he should lead the company and what he is *expected* to accomplish, compensation is not likely to be fairly related to performance.

In one company, the CEO annually prepares a one-page list of the major things he intends to accomplish in the next year. He reviews this with the compensation committee and the board, often receiving suggestions for change or clarification. A year later the CEO reviews this list with the committee to see how he has done. There are always a number of unanticipated developments during the year, but at least there is agreement at the beginning of the year and an assessment at year's end. This procedure gives the compensation committee a basis upon which to judge performance, and then to correlate it with compensation. Incidentally, the CEO of this company said that he kept the one-page list in the top drawer of his desk, and every few weeks, as he was making his plans, he checked the list to see where he stood. This helped remind him about areas in which some special effort was needed.

This method is probably not appropriate for all companies. We mention it here only to illustrate the thought process that should govern how the CEO and the compensation committee arrive at an understanding concerning expected accomplishments, and to demonstrate their relationship to the CEO's compensation. With such a method, it is unlikely that the CEO and the committee will be wildly at odds in their assessment of performance. Compensation adjustment will be properly understood and interpreted.

Competitive Range

The CEO's compensation should fall within a competitive range. If the CEO is doing a good job and the board does not want to lose him, the compensation committee needs to know what the competition is paying. Also, if the company wants to pay a premium over the market to the CEO, it should know roughly what that premium is and be comfortable that it is worthwhile. There is a plethora of survey information available—classified by industry, by size of company, and by geographical location—to enable the committee to get an idea of competitive compensation levels. And, the company's staff can compile information from the proxy statements of comparable companies. There are also many consulting organizations that can provide useful information. In the end, however, the committee must make its own judgment as to where in the competitive spectrum they want their CEO's compensation to fall.

A note of caution is in order for using data and salary information provided by consulting organizations. Careful distinctions need to be made between base salary, bonus, and compensation from incentive programs. If a sample is small, there can be significant distortions in the data resulting from a one-time exercise of options or a large payout from a long-term incentive program by one or a few CEOs. Moreover, if a company wants to pay its CEO at the 50th percentile, and if relatively few companies want to be below the average, the average is inevitably and mathematically forced higher and higher. Staying with the average, therefore, may lose some of its significance over time. Finally, it is important to remember that compensation consultants are usually hired by the CEO and can't help but know which side their bread is buttered on. There are, of course, many highly qualified consultants in the field of executive compensation, but one should be alert to the possibility of understandable bias.

Motivation

The third guideline is that the compensation arrangements should motivate the CEO to do what's expected of him. If the board wants him to move aggressively, to take unusual risks and not to be concerned with the possibility of near-term losses, it should structure a compensation plan that will reward that kind of behavior. One possibility would be a multiyear contract to provide assurance of employment during a high-risk phase, together with some type of long-term incentive, such as stock options that vest after three years and are exercisable over a 10-year period. At the other extreme, the conservative board of a mature company might be interested in moderate growth but secure dividends. An alternative in that case would be a compensation plan weighted largely in the direction of a fixed salary, reviewed annually, with only modest incentive features.

There are a wide variety of compensation arrangements, each of which provides some type of motivation: base salary reviewed annually; base salary plus annual discretionary bonus; base salary with bonus based on a formula; stock option plans; performance share plans; multiyear incentive plans; the list goes on and on. Benefits play an important part in CEO compensation arrangements, retirement programs in particular. In any event, each plan has its own motivational features, and it is important that the compensation committee structure a plan that will provide the kind of motivation for the CEO that the board wants to generate.

As a general rule, we believe that the compensation committee should be permitted to exercise a considerable degree of judgment in setting the CEO's compensation. The rigid application of formulas can produce anomalies in compensation—particularly bonuses—that may be unrelated to performance, that do not provide appropriate motivation, or that result in payments that are embarrassingly high. The advantage of the formula approach is that an executive can usually calculate his compensation. This takes the committee "off the hook" insofar as the exercise of judgment is concerned. We believe that compensation should be determined by an appropriate mix of formula and judgment.

Many compensation committees get locked into granting a bonus that is largely determined by formula and which may produce unrealistic results. For instance, when Archie McCardell joined International Harvester as chairman and CEO, part of the employment contract was that he would participate in an incentive plan which provided awards based on International Harvester's financial performance in comparison with certain competitors. Although the company was on the verge of bankruptcy when McCardell was terminated in 1982, he received an award of approximately $1 million under this plan. Industry sources said the reason for this large award was that Massey-Ferguson, one of the competitive companies against which International Harvester's performance was measured, underwent a major reorganization and reported a loss of over $400 million in 1982. This source added that if Massey-Ferguson's results had not been included in the formula for calculating the incentive award, McCardell would have received little, if anything, under the plan.

This example indicates how factors that cannot be fully anticipated can drastically distort compensation determined strictly by a formula. Thus, while recognizing that formulas have a place in determining compensation, we suggest that they be used cautiously. The board and the compensation committee should preserve a wide area for the exercise of judgment in establishing the compensation plan for the CEO.

COMPENSATION POLICY

It is important that every company have a policy—representing its philosophy—regarding executive compensation. This policy should come from, or at least be endorsed by, the board, and it should be consistently applied and widely understood. Some examples:

- Company A has a policy of paying its senior executive group on the average, at the 75th percentile for companies of similar size in its industry. With this policy, applied over a 15-year period, the company has attracted and retained a superior group of executives. The compensation committee of this board annually reviews the data on the company's position in relation to this standard. Several years ago the company fell behind, dropping to somewhere around the fiftieth percentile. Adjustments were made to bring average compensation back to policy levels.

- Company B has a policy of paying a relatively high percentage of total compensation in the form of bonus or incentive payments. Base pay is lower than customary in the industry, but when the company has a good year (i.e., when performance substantially exceeds budget), the executive group receives handsome bonuses. Under this policy, total pay for an executive is likely to fluctuate quite significantly from year to year. However, this policy is widely known and accepted within the company.

- Company C's compensation policy is actually a part of its overall employment philosophy, which includes pay levels at industry standards, participation in company profits, a superior benefit program, and no layoffs. This philosophy stems from that of the company's founders and is consistently applied throughout, from the senior executive level on down. This is a tough-minded, highly successful company in a high-technology industry. It is understandable that Company C is regarded as an extraordinarily fine place to work.

- Company D is a successful company in a highly cyclical, capital-intensive industry. Its senior executives are compensated with base pay at industry-average levels combined with a long-term incentive plan. The latter includes both stock options and a performance share plan with a three-year award period. Grants under the performance share plan are based on the company's average return on equity over the period.

These four companies have distinctly different compensation policies. However, in each the policies were designed to meet the particular needs of the company and its business. Moreover, since they are consistently applied and well understood, they become a part of the company's culture.

As we indicated earlier, executives are understandably sensitive when it comes to their compensation. Most of them think about it a good deal and are prone to speculate over the meaning of changes in the amount they receive. If there is no apparent policy—if there seems to be no rhyme or reason to compensation changes—an executive may get confusing and inconsistent signals. Why is my base pay up only 7 percent? Why wasn't my bonus larger? What does it take to get a decent increase around here? Are they suggesting that I start looking around? These interpretations, frequently wrong and unintended, can cause unrest and jeopardize motivation.

By contrast, a company policy helps to bring an element of consistency and predictability to compensation matters. A framework then exists that enables an executive to understand

and to interpret his compensation, thereby minimizing the chance of misunderstanding and possible frustration.

COMPENSATION REVIEWS

In addition to setting the CEO's compensation, the committee also determines compensation for the senior executive group. The number of executives varies from company to company, ranging from a few to 30 or more. This group usually includes the corporate officers and others whose salaries are above a specified level. Many companies conduct an annual review of the executive group with the compensation committee shortly after the close of the fiscal year, when the company's operating results are known. The company's senior personnel officer or human resources officer participates in the annual review, sometimes with an assistant or an outside consultant. Before the committee looks at individual compensation, these staff people may provide background information detailing the company's overall compensation history for the past several years, trends and expectations for the coming year, and how the company's compensation levels compare with industry averages.

Following the staff presentation, the CEO makes his recommendations for bonus and salary changes for the executive group (except for his own). Supporting information is also provided. This includes each individual's salary grade, the salary range for that grade, current salary, and date and percent of the last increase; proposed salary, effective date, and the amount and percent of increase; last year's bonus, proposed bonus, last year's salary plus bonus, and this year's salary plus bonus. If a company has a stock option, performance share or other incentive plan, there may be a separate schedule with appropriate data along with the CEO's recommendation. Each company develops its own format for presenting information to the compensation committee. The CEO provides explanations for his recommendations and responds to questions.

As a result of questions and the ensuing discussion, modest changes are sometimes made for a few people on the list. For the most part, however, the committee accepts the CEO's recommendations, since they are not in a position to evaluate individual performance. Of course, the CEO must provide reasonable and satisfactory explanations to the committee's questions. Although the committee does not ordinarily change the CEO's recommendations, its review process is important, as this provides a useful check on the CEO. Does he seem to be compensating people for the type of performance the board wants to see? Does he identify especially promising executives, and does he compensate them adequately? Does he seem to have reasonable equity and balance in the way he compensates his senior executives? These are just a few of the important questions the committee should ask, and it is good discipline for the CEO to answer them.

After completing the review of the CEO's recommendations, the committee excuses the CEO so that they can discuss *his* compensation. The company's top personnel or human resources officer and perhaps one of his analysts (or a consultant) might be asked to stay with the committee for a brief period to answer questions. The committee will usually have considerable competitive CEO salary data and information on salary trends. With this information, plus their knowledge of the company's financial results for the year, the committee can discuss and decide on the CEO's bonus for the previous year and his salary for the coming year. This recommendation, together with recommendations for the executive group, is reported to the full board, and after discussion, which is usually limited, the committee's recommendations are normally approved.

THE COMMITTEE'S DILEMMA

In this fairly typical process, the CEO's bonus and salary are set following the committee's review with the CEO of his recommendations for the executive group. This sometimes creates an awkward situation. For example, the CEO may recommend salary increases ranging from 5 percent to 15 percent, averaging 9 percent for his senior executives on the basis that the company has done well and that some executives have performed extremely well. When the compensation committee accepts this recommendation, it becomes more or less *locked in* with respect to the CEO's compensation. If the committee doesn't give the CEO at least a 9 percent raise, it will obviously communicate some dissatisfaction with his performance. Indeed, it can be argued that the CEO expects an increase as large as or larger than the highest he gave. From the committee's point of view, having the CEO make his recommendations before a decision is made on his own compensation complicates matters. The CEO is placed in the position of making his judgments without knowing the committee's own evaluation of senior management's performance. In a sense, this process puts the CEO on the spot, while at the same time inhibiting the discretion of the compensation committee.

To avoid this problem, one committee has adopted the practice of setting the CEO's bonus and salary one month ahead of the meeting at which the CEO makes his recommendations for the senior executive group. With this process, the CEO gets a sense of the committee's and the board's assessment of overall performance prior to making his recommendations. The arrangement has worked well for this company.

Not all compensation committee actions take place once a year. Some companies stagger salary changes throughout the year.

BENEFITS AND PERKS

Benefits—such as retirement programs, health benefits, savings plans, insurance—are clearly a part of overall compensation and thus, in most companies, come within the purview of the compensation committee. While these programs generally do not receive the degree of attention given to direct compensation matters, they do warrant regular review. Practices change frequently, and there are few fixed standards against which a company can measure its programs. However, as with other forms of compensation, the company must be competitive. The committee should therefore occasionally ask for a review of the company's program. This should not be done on a piecemeal basis. The benefits program is the sum of many separate features, and it is the total package that is important. Such a review will point out the extent to which the company's program is competitive and also reveal any deficiencies that require attention.

The compensation committee should be familiar with how the company communicates it policies on benefits to employees. There is wide variation in practice, and in many instances employees (including senior executives) do not realize the extent or value of all of the benefits they can or will receive under company-paid programs. In the aggregate the company's benefit programs constitute a very large expenditure and should be effectively communicated to all participants.

Executive perquisites have, in recent years, come under increasingly close scrutiny. In fact, SEC regulations currently require disclosure of the receipt of perquisites by an executive if their cash value exceeds $25,000 in a year. While most companies are prudent about perks, there are occasional excesses that violate good sense. Moreover, there are many borderline situations. For example, when the CEO is on a business trip with the company airplane and he takes a detour on his way home to stop and visit his son at college, to what degree is this personal as opposed to company expense?

Because executive perks can be a sensitive area, the company should have well-defined policies to protect both the company and the executives involved. The extent and nature of executive perks, as well as the policies governing their use, should be reviewed by either the compensation committee or the audit committee on a regular basis.

BOARD REMUNERATION

Another function of the compensation committee is to recommend to the full board the compensation arrangements for the board itself. Obviously, this is a delicate matter, since the board is disbursing company funds (actually shareowner funds) to itself.

Directors' compensation is disclosed in the annual proxy statement. Most companies would like to see their directors "respectably" compensated, and while compensation should not be the compelling reason for holding a directorship, directors want to feel that they are being compensated on a competitive basis. On the other hand, most directors want to feel confident that their compensation is not excessive and that they could never be exposed to criticism for improperly compensating themselves.

To help reach a balanced level of compensation, a good deal of survey information is available on corporate practices. These data are broken down by industry and by size of company. They include range and median information, the split between retainer and board meeting fees, compensation for committee chairmanship, and other relevant practices. With this information, the committee should first decide where it wants the company to be positioned in the compensation spectrum. One company may have a tradition of paying directors generously in relation to the average. Another, perhaps with earnings problems, might intentionally want directors' compensation to be on the low end of the spectrum. In any case, having decided where they want to be in the range, the committee should then instruct the company staff to track the survey data from year to year and to alert the committee when they believe a change is appropriate. The committee, of course, makes its recommendation to the full board, which then acts on the matter.

The Scott Company case, at the end of this chapter, deals with the issue of director compensation after retirement. This is not a common practice, and it has been questioned. Is it proper for a board to compensate board members who are no longer active?

Another, though infrequently used, method of compensating board members is to grant stock options. We doubt that this is a wise practice, as stock options are normally used for motivating management. Since management is in direct control of operations and can significantly influence corporate performance, options can be a powerful incentive. The board's position and function, however, is different. It does not directly influence corporate performance, at least in the near term, and thus it is inappropriate and not in the shareowners' interests to use options for the purpose of motivating the board. The single exception to this statement may be in the case of start-up or near start-up situations, where stock options might be the best way to attract directors who possess special capabilities needed by the company. Cash, which may be limited, might not be nearly as attractive to these directors as a chance to participate in significant growth. In these instances, an arrangement to pay directors with stock options may be quite justifiable. In the normal corporate situation, however, using options as a means of director compensation is not warranted.

HUMAN RESOURCES

In recent years, there has been a trend toward broadening the scope of the compensation committee, combining the responsibility for both compensation and human resources into a human resources committee. This arrangement is particularly applicable in people-intensive companies. The human resources committee—in addition to addressing compensation issues—reviews with management the adequacy of the company's programs that have been designed to provide the organizational capabilities needed to implement the corporate plan. These reviews will deal with such questions as:

- What are the company's future requirements for management personnel and other human resources, and are these requirements included in the company's long-range plan?

- Is there a suitable management development program in place to meet projected needs? How do we evaluate this program?
- What are the trends in employee turnover—and what employee categories have the highest turnover? Do the trends suggest inadequacies in compensation, working environment, or other areas?
- What are the company's recruiting programs? Results? Plans?
- What is the company's record in affirmative action and Equal Employment Opportunity programs?

As an increasing number of companies enter the service industries, which tend to be people oriented, these issues will become more important. Just as capital investment budgets have been, and are, carefully scrutinized by the board, it is likely that issues relating to human resources will become a more important subject of board concern.

CASE
Atlantic Corporation—When Is Enough Too Much?

Mike Morris, who in 1979 was 62 years old, was generally credited with saving the Atlantic Corporation. He had been recruited by the Atlantic board in 1969 as its chairman and CEO when the company was in serious difficulty. Profits had been declining for several years, and in 1969 product-quality problems had resulted in large write-offs that threatened the company's solvency. To complicate matters further, the technology of Atlantic's industry was changing rapidly and many of its products and plants were facing obsolescence. Many industry observers wondered whether or not Atlantic would survive.

To attract Morris, the Atlantic board proposed an attractive compensation package, including a salary and bonus that were competitive within the industry, a generous stock option plan, and a special benefits-and-retirement plan. Morris and the directors seemed comfortable with these arrangements and with the understanding that as the company progressed, Morris' compensation would be appropriately adjusted.

Morris moved quickly and effectively to reorganize the company. Over the course of the next several years, the product line was significantly revamped, a number of obsolete plants were closed, and the company's total employment was reduced by 25 percent. The company slowly returned to profitability, and by the late 1970s Atlantic had regained its position in its highly competitive industry. Prominent business and financial people were lavish in their praise of Morris's accomplishments.

During this period Morris's compensation was reviewed annually by the compensation committee. His salary was increased each year, he was granted additional stock options, and he also earned a substantial bonus related to company performance. The company regularly employed a consulting firm to help establish competitive compensation ranges for the executive organization. The senior member of this consulting organization reported to the compensation committee from time to time on the adequacy of Morris's arrangements. Based on these and other reports, the committee (and through the committee, the full board) believed that Morris's compensation was on the adequate to generous side.

As was customary, the committee met in January 1979 to consider Morris's recommendations for bonus, salary changes, and stock options for senior officers. This was also the time when the committee reviewed Morris's compensation. Morris sat with the committee until the time for discussion of his own compensation, at which time he left the room. Before leaving, however, he gave the committee members a brief report that had been prepared by the consulting organization, relating to his own compensation.

The report briefly summarized Morris's accomplishments over the previous decade, stressing that Atlantic's current condition was largely a result of his leadership. The report noted that Morris would retire in two more years under the company's mandatory age 65 retirement policy, and that his continued leadership was essential during this period. Finally, the consultant suggested that in light of Morris's extraordinary contributions to Atlantic, the board might want to make a somewhat unusual compensation arrangement for him over these final two years, both in recognition of his contributions and to assure that the company would benefit from his services during this period. The consultant indicated that a special payment (perhaps spread over two or more years) roughly equal to three or four times his annual salary could be justified.

The committee was surprised by this report. After some discussion, Morris was asked to return to the meeting. In response to questions, he explained that he had initiated the consultant's report because he had recently been approached by a financial group to take on a fast-developing new venture. He believed that this venture would almost certainly net him several million dollars in capital gains within a few years. He said that although his Atlantic salary and bonus had been adequate, his options had not worked out as he had hoped. While acknowledging that some of his early option grants had significant value, he added that the more recent awards, which were much larger than the earlier ones, had a disappointingly modest value. (This was true. The P/E ratio of securities for all companies in Atlantic's industry had declined and so stock prices had not increased proportionately to increases in earnings.)

As a result, Morris said he was nowhere near achieving his capital accumulation objective. He was aware that he had only a few more years of active management and that he did not want to let unusual opportunities slip by. Morris said that although he had a strong sense of loyalty to Atlantic, to both the board and the organization, he was not legally obligated to remain with the company. Moreover, given the way his retirement and other benefits were structured, there would be only minimal diminution resulting from early retirement. He also pointed out that previous Atlantic chairmen had retired as wealthy men, and he clearly implied that he had contributed at least as much—and in some cases considerably more—than his predecessors. (Most board members agreed with this observation.) In light of these several considerations, Morris hoped the committee and the board would look favorably on his request. Although no deadline was mentioned, it was clear that Morris expected a response soon.

The compensation committee had had no previous indication of Morris' dissatisfaction. The chairman, John Kircher, immediately arranged to hold an executive session with all the outside members of the board to inform them of this development and to discuss the appropriate course of action. At that time there were nine outside directors; four of them were either CEOs or senior executives of major corporations. The other outsiders were an investment banker, a commercial banker, a retired university professor, a lawyer, and a foundation president.

One of the principal concerns immediately expressed by some of the board members was the problem of succession. The company's president and chief operating officer was the obvious successor. He had been hired into this position five years earlier from a competing firm, as a backup and potential successor to Morris. The board was satisfied with him, and there was every expectation that he would become the chairman and CEO upon Morris's retirement two years hence.

Several board members, however, had serious reservations as to whether he was ready to succeed Morris at this time. In particular, they pointed out that if the current president became chairman immediately, there was no clear successor for him. Several younger executives in the second level of management were in the testing process, and it was expected that one would emerge in a year or two as an obvious candidate for the position. Making the change at this time would not permit this process to run its normal course.

In the lengthy executive session discussion, it developed that there was a wide range of views. Everyone was personally fond of Morris and had high regard for his accomplishments with Atlantic. Nevertheless, some felt uncomfortable with Morris' proposal and thought that it would be basically wrong for the board to agree to his request. They believed that Morris had a responsibility to complete his program, leading to succession in two years, and that his compensation had been and continued to be generous. Others were willing to accommodate his request, fearing that his departure at this time would have a serious impact on the company. Moreover, they pointed out that with profits now running at more than $200 million a year, a pre-tax payment to Morris of even a couple of million dollars spread over several years would have an almost imperceptible effect on earnings.

The result of this meeting was inconclusive, and it was clear that there were divergent and strongly held views. It was agreed only that Kircher should meet again with Morris and that another executive session of the outside board members should be convened at the next regular monthly board meeting.

Kircher wondered how to proceed.

Discussion of the Case

The Atlantic Corporation case was read by four persons, each of whom was also a senior officer of a large company and each of whom had considerable experience as directors. This was followed by a spirited discussion, which is summarized below:

Joe: I don't see any big problem. Make the deal with Morris. It's peanuts so far as the company is concerned—and besides, for saving the company he deserves it. In addition, the board doesn't really have any good options, since his successor isn't ready. I say, pay him and get on with it.

Sam: You really shock me, Joe. How in the world can you justify agreeing to pay Morris two million dollars just because he's asked for it? He's been competitively compensated as chairman and CEO and that's all anyone can ask. To do more is to violate the trust of the shareowners. The fact that he hasn't gotten wealthy because of his stock options is not the board's fault. Morris has to take the stock-market risk along with everyone else. Besides, who is to know that the value of his options won't zoom up in the next couple of years? I think the board has done the proper thing and it shouldn't change its deal with Morris. It's a matter of principle. If he leaves, he leaves.

Joe: Yes, but what happens then? The board is left with a successor and second-level management neither of which is in shape to carry on. I still don't think the directors have any reasonable alternative—in the shareowners' interest—but to agree to Morris's terms.

Bill: I hear both of you—but I just wonder if the president is really as unprepared to step up to the CEO job as you suggest, Joe. We're all on several boards, and each of us has seen transitions from one CEO to another. Have you ever been totally confident that the new man was fully prepared to take over the top job? Isn't there always a risk—no matter how long or how well prepared the successor is? Look, Morris's successor has been around for five years as chief operating officer, he's done a good job and the board is impressed with him—what more do you want?

Sam: You're making sense, Bill. After all, this is a free country and if Morris wants to accept the offer, let him do it. The board will have to take its chances with the president. They're just doing it a couple of years early. That's all. Don't you agree, Dick? You haven't said anything yet.

Dick: No, I haven't. The reason is I've just been wondering if we're not missing something here. The case points out very clearly that there were widely and strongly held views among the board members, as there are here. Kircher, as compensation committee chairman, has been given the responsibility by the board to do something. Right? Well, it seems to me that high on the list of things he should be concerned with is preventing members of the board from becoming too polarized over this issue. A smooth-working and compatible board is an important organizational asset. It seems to me that if Kircher went to the next board meeting proposing either Joe's or Sam's position (perhaps having previously discussed it with Morris), he would run a real risk of damaging relationships within the board. Don't you think he should be sensitive to this possibility?

Joe: I guess you're right, Dick. You sure would like to avoid having a split board over this problem. Whatever happens, the board should be together—either backing a new CEO or agreeing on terms with Morris.

Dick: Yes. And this suggests to me that a compromise of some sort should be reached before people paint themselves into corners. At least it would be worth trying.

Sam: I understand what you're saying, Dick—but that might not be so easy to accomplish. Just what do you do?

Dick: Well, on the assumption that it is important to preserve the board's working relationship, it seems to me that I would try to arrange for each board member to have an opportunity, privately, to express himself on the subject. This would take some time on Kircher's part—maybe too much. Perhaps he should ask a couple of other board members to help him—or even retain an outside professional. But everyone should have a chance to be heard. Out of these discussions Kircher could get a sense of what the board might support as a middle ground. This might take another discussion at an executive session of the board—but at least there is a chance that consensus could be reached. I think Kircher should give something like that a try before making a decision one way or another.

Bill: I understand what you're driving at, Dick, but do you really think this is a situation in which a compromise is appropriate? Aren't there matters of principle involved?

Dick: Sure there are, Bill, but in the end I personally would like to see an outcome that would keep Morris with the company until retirement, preserve the board's working relationship, and still not offend any individual board member's sense of principle. This is what I'm working for. You've all seen enough of these situations to realize that out of the give and take of discussion, good solutions can be reached—solutions that are sometimes better than those any individual has suggested. It is this process—at the board level—that is needed, and Kircher is in a position to initiate it. If he does, I'd be willing to bet that the board would agree to a range of acceptable solutions and that Morris, realizing that his board is acting in concert, would agree to a compromise arrangement. He'd probably like to get the whole matter settled, anyway, and get on with business.

Sam: Sounds good to me.

Atlantic Corporation Addendum.   In this case, Kircher, after consulting several board members, hired an experienced consultant in whom he had confidence. Over the ensuing two weeks the consultant talked with each outside board member and with Morris. He concluded that a reasonable compromise was possible, based on a substantial final option grant for Morris. Kircher checked the proposal with several board members and obtained a favorable response. At the executive session of the outside board members (with the consultant present) the proposal was quickly agreed upon. Kircher then met briefly with Morris, and the episode was closed.

Everyone was relieved, and this matter was never mentioned again.

Our Comment on Atlantic Corporation

The situation with Mike Morris, while unusual, does highlight the importance that a CEO can attach to his compensation. While Morris had not previously indicated dissatisfaction, the company obviously had a vulnerability of which it was unaware. Perhaps if there had been more frequent and informed dialogue between Morris and Kircher, the almost head-on conflict might have been avoided.

This case also shows how people having different backgrounds can have honestly held differing views of compensation matters. Some board members were not particularly concerned about a $2 million payment to Morris, while others believed it was improper. It is not hard to understand that a partner of a successful, private New York investment banking firm might not consider an extra $2 million payment to be excessive, in light of Morris's accomplishments over a 10-year period. In good years, the partners of successful investment banks receive this much and more—in some instances, good-sized multiples of this amount. On the other hand, through the eyes of a director from the educational community, such compensation might understandably appear too high. It is good for a board to have such diversity. It assures that important decisions will not be made without considering the viewpoints of the varying constituencies of the corporation. In this respect, Atlantic had a good board.

In this instance, reaching a decision that could be supported by the outside directors was especially important. They were dealing not simply with a compensation issue, but potentially with succession to the CEO position. There is no more important decision that a board can make; if the directors were split and could not agree on an arrangement that would retain Morris, his successor might be taking over without the full support of the board. In fact, whether Morris stayed or left, there was a good chance that the board's relationship with either him or his successor would be strained. These possibilities were certainly of major concern to Kircher.

We believe that Kircher acted wisely in arranging for each board member to have an opportunity to discuss his feelings with an objective third party. This, together with some time, helped defuse the situation. It also made it possible to search for areas of compromise. That the matter was quickly resolved at the next meeting and never again mentioned suggests that the company successfully avoided a crisis and retained a good working board with constructive relations with its chairman and CEO.

Finally, the Atlantic case illustrates the pivotal role that the compensation committee plays in the work of a board of directors. In dealing with the CEO's compensation, the committee not only sets the compensation standard for the company, but deals with one of the board's most sensitive issues. A good compensation committee has a sense of perspective and feeling for diplomacy that enables it to navigate some uncertain, and sometimes troubled, waters.

CASE

Scott Company—Has the Favor Been Earned?

Hugh Grady, an outside director of Scott Company, found himself in a situation that, although of trivial financial importance to the company, was of considerable personal concern.

At the February 1983 meeting, the compensation committee recommended that directors be paid a pension after their retirement. The annual pension would be equal to the director's retainer fee in the year he retired and would be paid for the number of years that the director had been on the board, until the year of the retiree's death or for a period of ten years, whichever came sooner. The proposal did not contemplate pensions for the two living retired directors. They had the status of "honorary," could attend meetings, but could not vote. None of them was present at the February meeting.

The proposal was brought up by the CEO. It was made at that particular time because a highly respected, but not wealthy, director would reach the mandatory retirement age of 70 at the annual meeting in May 1983; part of the rationale was that this would be a way of showing the company's appreciation for his many contributions. This director was present at the meeting.

Grady was president of a university, age 67 with no substantial amount of accumulated savings. His annual Scott Company pension, under the proposed plan, would be about one third of the pension he expected to receive from the university upon his retirement three years hence. He was not aware of this proposal until the compensation committee made its report at the board meeting. He therefore had only a few minutes in which to decide how he would vote on this proposal.

Outside directors of Scott Company received an annual retainer, a fee for attendance at board meetings, and a fee for attendance at committee meetings. From time to time, these amounts were compared with published data for companies of similar size and companies in the same industry (data on size within industry were not available). The practice was to maintain the retainer and fees at approximately the bottom of the upper quartile of comparable companies. Changes were made every two or three years. The four inside directors received no additional compensation for their activities as directors. The compensation of the CEO was comparable to the highest CEO compensation in the industry, partly because he was doing an outstanding job.

In introducing the proposal, the chairman of the compensation committee said that although the practice of paying pensions to outside directors was relatively new, it was spreading rapidly. He quoted a recent survey, which showed that 13 percent of the Fortune 500 industrials had retirement arrangements for outside directors, more than twice the percentage in 1980.

In 1982, Scott Company earnings were at a record high. The cost of the pension was, of course, trivial compared with earnings but would build somewhat in later years.

Grady was convinced that a pension (or indeed any aspect of compensation) was not necessary to attract the caliber of directors that the company needed. Although not all ten outside directors were wealthy, the level of compensation probably had not influenced their decision to join the board, or to remain on it. However, there was a feeling that Scott Company's regard for its directors was indicated by their compensation, and that the amount should therefore be competitive.

Grady felt that few, if any, directors would oppose the recommendation, and that if he did so, he would be regarded as a maverick, at best. He had not made up his mind when the discussion began. The first question was whether the facts about the directors' pension would be disclosed in the proxy statement, and the answer was yes. The next question was about a possible pension for directors already retired, and the answer was that a retroactive pension might present legal problems. There was then a pause, and the chairman was ready to call for a vote.

Our Comment on Scott Company

Pensions for directors raise sensitive issues. Conscientious directors are uncomfortable when placed in self-serving positions where they must vote to give themselves benefits. They want to be certain that what they are doing is proper and that they are not subject to criticism of misusing their positions to receive unjust enrichment.

On the surface, the proposed Scott Company pension appears quite generous. In Grady's case it would supplement his university pension significantly. He was presumably concerned about the propriety of voting for the pension proposal. Would he be acting purely out of self-interest, or was this truly in the best interest of the Scott Company shareowners? That the proposal was sprung at the last minute, with a single retiring director in mind, probably also troubled Grady. And rightfully so.

The size of the increase in total director compensation that the pension proposal represented would be important in deciding whether or not to support the proposal. Apparently, no such information was provided. The present value of the pension would vary between directors, but it would have been helpful for the compensation committee to provide some ranges. For example, would the pension result in an increase in the 10 percent range or in the 40 percent range? The answer to this question makes a difference, especially if a director is concerned about the self-enrichment issue in the first place. The evidence suggests that Scott paid its directors quite well, and a large added pension increment might (and maybe should) make some directors uncomfortable. In any event, it appears that the board (and perhaps the committee as well) was not furnished with adequate information to make their decision.

It is unfortunate that there was pressure to deal with the pension recommendation immediately. Sometimes there are emergencies when decisions simply will not wait. But it is frustrating to a conscientious director to feel that he is obliged to vote on a matter that is not particularly pressing when he may want to have more information or more time to sort out his own thoughts. It would have been better to present the pension proposal informally at this meeting, providing an opportunity for discussion and questions, and indicating that the board would be asked to vote on it at the next meeting.

But Grady must vote now. An affirmative vote would be based on his confidence in the compensation committee. If his past experience has led him to have a high level of confidence, he might accept its recommendation. His other alternatives are to vote no, abstain, or suggest that the decision be deferred for one month. None of the alternatives is very palatable. In the end we would probably go along with the recommendation but make our concerns known to the CEO privately. (And this is what Grady actually did.)

It is unfortunate that neither the CEO nor the chairman of the compensation committee was aware of Grady's and perhaps other directors' sensitivities in this area so that the proposal could have been managed differently.

We have nothing else to say on this touchy issue. One purpose of this case, however, is to ask the reader to think about the balance of a director's obligations to, and relationship with (1) the shareowners and society, (2) other directors, (3) the CEO, and (4) himself. Your reaction will be highly personal and will indicate your feelings about the nature of a director's responsibility.

7
The Audit Committee

An increasingly important function of the board of directors is to make certain that the company's published financial statements are fairly presented, that they are in conformance with generally accepted accounting principles, and that the company's control system is effective. Emphasis on the board's responsibility in this area began in the 1970s. This emphasis led to the creation of audit committees in companies that did not have them and in expanded duties of these committees in most companies. Both the New York and the American stock exchanges now require listed companies to have audit committees composed of outside directors.

DIRECTORS' RESPONSIBILITIES

Although the full board can delegate certain functions to its committees, this delegation does not relieve individual board members of their ultimate responsibility. In its 1967 decision in the BarChris case, the Federal court emphasized this fact:

Section 11 [of the Securities Act of 1933] imposes liability in the first instance upon a director, no matter how new he is. . . . He is presumed

*to know his responsibility when he became a director. He can escape
liability only by using that reasonable care to investigate the facts which
a prudent man would employ in the management of his own property.*

In the 1975 Stirling Homex case (Release 34-11514), the SEC
publicly criticized two outside directors, even though neither apparently had personal knowledge of the fact that the financial
statements were false and misleading.

Most companies have directors' and officers' (D&O) liability
insurance. This insurance is not, however, an absolute protection from claims, including legal costs, arising from lawsuits.
Lloyd Stauder, vice president and general counsel of Warnaco,
Inc., told his board (only slightly facetiously): "D&O insurance
protects you from everything except the one thing you probably
are going to get sued for." Although the situation varies from
state to state, it is generally believed that the insurance companies will pay if the director is found not to have acted in the
company's best interest, or if he was negligent.[1] Even if they are
indemnified, defense of a suit involves a loss of personal time,
publicity, and the likelihood of injury to the directors' reputations.

Suits against directors and officers are not rare. In 1982 the
Wyatt Company studied the experience of 1979 companies that
had D&O insurance. It reported that 300 of these companies filed
claims under their policies and that 40 percent of these resulted
from actions initiated by shareowners, with "misleading representation" being the most prominent allegation. The estimated
average cost of the 39 percent of claims for which payments were
made (including both claim cost and legal defense fees) was $1.3
million. Moreover, the cost of D&O insurance coverage is rising
rapidly, and some insurance companies will not write policies at
any price. (*Institutional Investor*, August 1985 reported that "almost overnight, two thirds of the industry's underwriting capac-
ity has vanished, and the erosion continues.")

[1]For a useful article on this topic, see Joseph W. Bishop, Jr., "Understanding
D&O Insurance Policies," *Harvard Business Review*, March–April 1978, p. 20.

Some directors take comfort in the business judgment rule, which says in effect that the courts will not ordinarily second-guess the business judgment that directors used in arriving at their decisions. Recent decisions suggest that the courts are increasingly willing to examine directors' decisions. The most chilling is the 1985 decision of the Delaware supreme court that the directors of Trans Union Corp. acted too hastily and without sufficient information in approving the sale of the company to another group. The directors settled out of court for $23.5 million, of which only $10 million was covered by D&O insurance.

AUDIT COMMITTEE RESPONSIBILITIES

In its judgment on the Killearn Properties, Inc., case (Litigation Release 6792), the SEC detailed the responsibilities of the audit committee. In our view, the principal responsibilities are the following:

- To ensure that the published financial statements are not misleading.
- To ensure that internal controls are adequate.
- To follow up on allegations of material, financial, ethical and legal irregularities.
- To ratify the selection of the external auditor.

The way in which the committee carries out each of these duties is discussed in the following sections. As will be seen, the committee's work occasionally leads to differences of opinion with the CEO that are second in importance only to the compensation matters discussed in Chapter 6.

Obviously, the audit committee does not directly conduct audits. It relies on two other audit groups to do this. One is the outside auditor, certified public accountants that all listed corporations are required to engage and that most other corporations do engage in order to satisfy the requirements of banks and other lenders. The other group is the firm's internal audit staff, company employees who report to a senior officer, often the CEO or chief financial officer. As discussed below, the work of these two groups overlaps in some respects.

PUBLISHED FINANCIAL STATEMENTS

The outside auditor gives an opinion regarding the published financial statements. As the standard form of opinion letter emphasizes, management, not the auditor, is responsible for the statements. In a clean opinion—the type that most companies seek and receive—the auditor says only that the statements "present fairly" the performance and status of the company in accordance with generally accepted accounting principles; the auditor does not say whether different numbers would have been even more fair. The audit committee's task is to decide whether the directors should concur with the outside auditor's opinion (or occasionally to resolve differences if the auditors are unwilling to give a clean opinion on the numbers that management proposes).

Management has some latitude in deciding on the amounts to be reported, especially the amount of earnings. Since managers are human beings, it is reasonable to expect them to lean in the direction of reporting performance in a favorable light. This tendency is seen principally in (1) the smoothing of earnings, (2) a reluctance to disclose borderline cases of unfavorable developments, and (3) "the big bath." Each of these is discussed below.

Smoothing Earnings

There is a widespread belief that the ideal performance is a steady growth in earnings, certainly from year to year, and desirably from quarter to quarter (although there is little hard evidence that short-run fluctuations in earnings have much, if any, effect on stock prices). Within the latitude permitted by generally accepted accounting principles, therefore, management may desire to smooth reported earnings. The principal techniques for doing this are to vary the adjustments for inventory amounts, for bad debts and for returns, allowances, and warranties. These adjustments and allowances are matters of judgment, and the auditors are not in a position to question the judgment of management, unless the case is fairly open and shut. (The amount of the pension liability is also a matter of judgment, but this amount is usually established by outside actuaries, and management accepts their written estimate.)

The audit committee therefore pays considerable attention to the calculation of these adjustments and allowances, and to the accounts receivable, inventory and accrued liability amounts that result from them. Changes in the reserve percentages from one year to the next are suspect. Within limits, the audit committee tolerates a certain amount of smoothing; indeed, they may not even be aware that smoothing has occurred. Outside these limits, however, the committee is obligated to make sure that the reserve and accrual calculations are reasonable.

Not all attempts to smooth earnings are unethical. For example, there are documented stories of division managers who have personally worked around the clock at year end, loading goods into United Parcel Service containers. This enabled the managers to count the goods in the containers as revenue in the year that was about to end. Counting as revenues goods that actually have been shipped is legitimate. By contrast, certain division managers at H.J. Heinz counted millions of dollars' worth of items as revenues even though the goods had not been shipped. This practice was wrong and, when uncovered, led to unfavorable publicity, an SEC investigation, and punishment.

Reporting Unfavorable Developments

The SEC requires that a report (Form 8-K) be filed promptly whenever an unusual material event that affects the financial statements becomes known. The principal concern is with the bottom line, the amount of reported earnings. Management, understandably, may be inclined not to report events that *might* (but also might not) have an unfavorable impact on earnings—the possible bankruptcy of an important customer; an apparent inventory shortage; a cash shortage that could turn out to be a bookkeeping error; a possibly defective product that could lead to huge returns or to product liability suits; possible safety or environmental violations; an IRS or Customs challenge that may turn out not to have a sound foundation; pending legal action that could have serious consequences. It is human nature to hope that borderline situations will not actually have a material impact.

Furthermore, publicizing some of these situations may harm the company unnecessarily. Disclosure of a legal filing against the company may be necessary; disclosure of the amount the company thinks it might lose in such litigation, in a report that the plaintiff can read, would be foolish. Both management and the audit committee have difficulty deciding which items should be reported on a Form 8-K or its equivalent.

In any event, the committee should be kept fully informed about all events that *might* eventually require filing a Form 8-K. One might think that management would welcome the opportunity to inform and thereby to shift part of the responsibility to the board, but managers, like most human beings, tend not to talk about bad news if there are reasonable grounds for withholding it.

Occasionally, a management may attempt to cook the books, that is, to manufacture favorable results by making entries that are not in accordance with accounting principles. The Stirling Homex case is a prominent example; management reported sales revenue for 10,000 of its modular homes, even though 9,100 of these homes were still in inventory. The audit committee must rely on the auditors (or occasionally on a whistle blower) to detect these situations.

The Big Bath

New management may "take a big bath"; that is, it may write off or write down assets in the year in which it takes over. These charges reduce the amounts of costs that remain to be charged off in future periods and hence make the reported incomes of future periods higher than they otherwise would be. Since the situation which led to the replacement of the former management may justify some such charge-offs, and since the directors don't want to disagree with the new CEO during the honeymoon period, this tactic is often tolerated. If, in future years, the inflated earnings lead to extraordinarily high bonuses, the board may come to regret its inaction.

Audit Committee Actions

In probing for the possible existence of any of these situations, the committee takes two approaches. First, on its own initiative, it asks certain questions of management: Why has the inventory reserve changed? Why has the receivables reserve changed? What is the rationale for large write-offs? Second, and much more importantly, the committee asks hard questions of both the outside auditor and the internal audit staff, designed to bring possible shortcomings to light.

The audit committee usually meets privately with the outside auditors and tells them, in effect: "If you have any doubts about the numbers, or if you have reason to believe that management has withheld material information, let us know. If you don't inform us, the facts will almost certainly come to light later on. When they do, you will be fired."

A more polite way of probing is to ask questions such as

- Is there anything more you would like to tell us?
- What were your biggest areas of concern?
- What were the most important matters, if any, on which you

and the company differed? (If some issue was settled on the grounds that the amount was not material, and the question of materiality was a borderline one, ask that this issue be explained fully.)

- Did the accounting treatment of certain events differ from general practice in the industry? If so, what is the rationale for the difference?
- How would you rate the professional competence of the finance and accounting staff?

Similar questions are asked of the head of the internal audit staff, also in a private meeting with the audit committee.

Usually these questions are raised orally. Since the auditors know from past experience what to expect, they come prepared to answer them. Some audit committees state their questions in writing. In Martin Marietta, for example, the chairman of the audit committee provides a list of questions to the outside auditors. He also asks the director of internal auditing to state in writing that, except for matters brought to the attention of the committee, nothing came to his attention about which the committee should have been informed. He asks the general counsel for a written statement on the status of pending litigation. He asks the chief financial officer to furnish a number of detailed schedules, including sizable loans and advances to officers and employees, contingent liabilities, expense accounts of officers and directors, payments of professional services, details on corporate overhead, and several others.

Although cases of inadequate disclosure make headlines, they occur in only a tiny fraction of one percent of listed companies. Most such incidents reflect poorly on the work of the board of directors and its audit committee. Increasingly, the courts are penalizing the boards involved for their laxness. Directors should ponder this fact: When serious misdeeds surface, the CEO often leaves the company, but the directors must stay with the ship and endure public criticism and the blot on their professional reputations. Their lives would be much more pleasant if they had acted promptly!

Quarterly Reports

Another SEC filing is Form 10-Q which contains a quarterly summary of key financial data. The audit committee does not need to review this report routinely. A good rule is that if some unusual situation affects the quarterly numbers, management should inform the chairman of the committee. The chairman should then decide either to let the report be published as proposed, or, if the topic seems sufficiently important, to discuss it by telephone with members of the committee.

INTERNAL CONTROL

In addition to its opinion on the financial statements, the outside auditor writes a *management letter*. This letter lists possible weaknesses in the company's control system that have come to the auditor's attention, together with recommendations for correcting the situation. (In the boilerplate preceding this list, the auditor disclaims responsibility for a complete analysis of the system; the listed items are only those that the firm happened to run across.) Internal auditors also write reports on the subject.

Most audit committees follow up on these reports by asking management to respond to the criticisms. If management disagrees with the recommended course of action, its rationale is considered and either accepted or rejected. If action is agreed to, the committee keeps the item on its agenda until it is satisfied that the matter has been resolved.

The audit committee has an especially difficult problem with internal audit reports. In the course of a year, even a moderate-size staff may write a hundred or more reports. Many of them are too trivial to warrant the committee's attention. (One of us recently participated in an audit committee meeting of a multibillion dollar entity in which 15 minutes was spent discussing a recommendation for an improvement in paperwork processing that was expected to save $24,000 annually.) However, drawing a line between important reports and trivial ones is difficult. A rule of thumb, such as "Tell us about the dozen most important matters," may be used, but it does not allow for the possibility that the thirteenth matter may also warrant committee attention.

In its private meeting with the head of internal audit, the audit committee assures itself that the internal audit staff has complete freedom to do its work. The committee also makes it clear that the head of internal audit has direct access to the audit committee chairman if a situation that may warrant board attention is uncovered. The internal auditor would normally report the matter in question to his superior first, but his primary obligation is to the audit committee. The committee in turn should guarantee as well as it can that the internal auditor will be fully protected against possible retaliation.

A particularly touchy problem is the audit of senior management's travel and entertainment expenses. Typically, the external auditor investigates whether the amounts claimed were actually spent, but not whether the expenses were reasonable. Only a relatively fearless internal audit organization would probe deeply into this topic on its own initiative. In a few companies, an audit committee member personally examines the expense vouchers of senior management. More commonly, every few years the committee instructs either the outside auditor or the internal audit staff to make such an examination; since the work is done at the express instruction of the committee, management is likely to cooperate. An ineffective audit committee avoids this problem entirely.

The committee also considers the adequacy of the internal audit organization. Is it large enough? Does it have the proper level of competence; for example, does someone know how to audit a computer system? In many companies the internal audit organization is a training ground where promising persons are groomed for controllership responsibilities. The audit committee may find it useful to get acquainted with the internal audit staff, as a basis for judging future candidates for the controller organization.

When campaigns to reduce overhead are undertaken, the internal audit staff may be cut more than is healthy for the organization. The committee should question such cuts and ask the outside auditor for his opinion on their desirability. (Since internal auditors do much of the verifying that otherwise would be done by external auditors, and at a lower cost per hour, external auditors may not have an unbiased view of the proper size of the internal audit organization, however.)

INVESTIGATIONS

In 1977, passage of the Foreign Corrupt Practices Act (FCPA) led to a focus on illegal, and legal but unethical, practices. In addition to foreign corrupt practices as such, the FCPA also requires that the accounting records should accurately reflect transactions and states that the company must have an adequate set of internal controls. Since senior management could conceivably engage in or condone these practices, the board of directors had to accept direct responsibility for ensuring compliance with the Act. Many boards did so by hiring outside law or auditing firms to investigate practices throughout the organization. Although the cost of such investigations was considerable, most boards decided that there was no alternative. (Hence, the FCPA Act is sometimes labelled the "lawyer and accountants relief act.") In the great majority of cases, nothing of consequence was uncovered. The FCPA has not in fact led to much action. As of March 1983, the SEC had initiated only 21 actions, and most of these related to failure to report perquisites, alteration of records, or inadequate internal controls; few were related to what most people think of as corrupt practices, that is, bribery.

As a legacy to the initial furor, many companies wrote good policy statements outlawing questionable practices covered by the Foreign Corrupt Practices Act. Also, managers at all levels were required to certify, annually or biannually, in writing, that they had adhered to these policies. The danger is that as time passes these certifications may become merely a paperwork exercise.

Possible violations of these policies may be uncovered. When this happens, the audit committee has a difficult task. As a practical matter, certain types of bribery are tolerated, especially in developing countries. (And even in the United States, giving the head waiter $5 in order to obtain a preferred table is not regarded as a sin.) Certain forms of contributions to politicians or other influential people are regarded as proper (meals, plane trips); others are legal but perhaps unethical (certain ways of channeling funds to politicians), and still others are clearly wrong (significant bribes). We do not make judgments on these matters. We do suggest that the audit committee, and indeed the board as a whole, should develop an attitude toward them, communicate this attitude to management by words and deeds, and not forget about their policy as time goes on.

The company's house counsel is usually involved in investigating alleged violations of the Foreign Corrupt Practices Act and other improprieties. Some audit committees therefore meet privately with counsel, separately from its meetings with the external and internal auditors. Arjay Miller suggests that these questions be asked

- Are you telling us all we should know?
- Are you in a position to know what you should know?
- Is the committee doing what it should with the information it has?

STAFF ASSISTANCE

A few people believe that the audit committee should be supported by a full-time staff. Arthur Goldberg, former Supreme Court Justice, resigned from the TWA board because management would not grant his request for such assistance. We doubt that in normal circumstances full-time staff assistance is necessary; the board should rely on company employees for necessary help.

In those unusual circumstances where there may be a conflict of interest between board members and management, the board should of course engage outside counsel or outside accountants. Investigations made to ensure compliance with the Foreign Corrupt Practices Act and investigations dealing with serious allegations about the conduct of senior management are examples. These outside advisors ordinarily report to the chairman of the audit committee.

SELECTION OF AUDITORS

Ordinarily, management recommends that the current auditing firm be appointed for another year and that a proposed audit scope and fee schedule be adopted. The audit committee, perhaps after some questioning, agrees to the proposed scope and fee schedule and routinely recommends that the board (and subsequently, the shareowners) approve the selection of auditors. Occasionally, the audit committee needs to give more than routine consideration to this topic.

Large public accounting firms, as a matter of policy, rotate personnel assigned to a particular audit engagement to avoid the possibility that its staff will become too friendly with company personnel. If the company's outside auditor does not have this policy, the audit committee should insist on a rotation.

There also may be advantages to changing auditors, even when the relationship between the firm and the company has been satisfactory for a period of years, if for no other reason than that the possibility of obtaining bids from other firms may cause the current firm to think carefully about its proposed fees. However, the public may perceive a change in outside auditors as evidence that the superseded firm would not go along with a practice that the company wanted. The SEC, in fact, requires that if new auditors are appointed, the reason for making the change must be reported on a Form 8-K. Also, a new firm's initial task of learning about the company requires management time, and management may be reluctant to initiate a change for this reason.

If a new firm is engaged, there must be an understanding that the engagement will be for some minimum period, such as three years, even though the auditors are technically appointed annually. Otherwise, the extra time required in the first year to learn about the company cannot be justified.

Public accounting firms often perform nonaudit work for the company, and it is not uncommon for the compensation for this work to exceed the compensation for audit work. Recently, some people have criticized this practice. In the early 1980s, the SEC, responding to Congressional pressure, expressed doubts about its propriety. The critics point out that if the auditors install a system, participate in the evaluation of assets in an acquisition, or develop a buy-out proposal, they cannot be expected to criticize their own work during the subsequent audit. We see little evidence that this criticism is valid. The people in an accounting firm who do nonaudit work are usually not the same people who perform the audit. They can, however, obtain useful information from the audit partner, which helps them do a better job.

Nevertheless, the fact that audit fees are paid by the client creates subtle pressures. Moreover, the nonaudit work is carried out by a partner other than the auditing partner, and the nonaudit partner may be unhappy if an engagement is lost because of management dissatisfaction with the financial audit. The leading firms are fully aware of the pressures that exist and of the perception by some people that with the present method of compensation they cannot truly be independent. There seems to be no satisfactory alternative, however.

CONCLUSION

Audit committee members have a touchy job. On the one hand, as directors they want to support the CEO—the person whom the board itself selected. On the other hand, they have a clear responsibility to uncover and act on management inadequacies. If they do not do so, they, along with the rest of the board, are at the very least subject to criticism, and at worst they may ultimately wind up in jail. Their task is neither easy nor pleasant.

In discharging its duties, the audit committee must rely heavily on the outside auditors and the internal audit staff, and in some circumstances on the company's house counsel. This does not mean that the committee waits for these parties to come to it; rather, it schedules regular meetings with them, asks hard questions, is not satisfied until corrective action has been taken on problems that are uncovered, and makes it clear that these parties are ultimately responsible to the committee, not to management. The CEO, for his part, must be careful not to give the impression that he is trying to dominate the work of the committee.

CASE
Tanner Corporation—A System Breakdown

John Bentwood, chairman of the audit committee of the board of directors of Tanner Corporation was considering whether he should support a proposed change in the committee's relationship with company employees. This change was initiated as the result of an unfortunate incident that had occurred recently in the process systems division. The change was designed to increase the committee's ability to find out what was going on in the company.

Tanner Corporation was a large, diversified company organized into 31 operating divisions. The company had operated profitably for many years, and had expanded steadily, through both internal growth and acquisitions. In 1975 its sales revenue was approximately $900 million. Its board of directors had 12 members: 9 outside directors; plus Seth Remick, president and chairman of the board; Fred Thompson, executive vice president; and Spencer Brody, financial vice president.

The Audit Committee.   The audit committee was created in 1972. At that time, there was a general movement in publicly held corporations to set up such committees. In 1975, the committee consisted of four members:

John Bentwood, chairman, partner in a management consulting firm, and a certified public accountant with extensive experience in accounting and control systems.

Francis Dube, a lawyer whose firm had no connection with the company.

George Springer, senior vice president of a large manufacturing company.

Guy Hamel, executive vice president of Tanner Corporation's principal commercial bank.

Hamel had been elected to the board in 1973 and became a member of the audit committee in 1974. The other three members had been directors for many years and were original members of the audit committee.

Process Systems Division.   In 1971 Tanner acquired a small company whose management had developed a new technology for automating a variety of chemical production processes. The process systems division was an outgrowth of this acquisition. The division first developed a general approach to process automation for a given industry, with heavy emphasis on special purpose computers. It contracted with individual firms in that industry to adapt this general approach to the firm's specific needs and to install an automated system. It built many of the components required for the new systems, adapted other components, and purchased still other components. Each contract was for at least $100,000, and most were much larger.

In the first year, customers were hard to find, but after a few successful installations, sales volume increased. It doubled from 1972 to 1973 and more than doubled again in 1974. Because of development costs and the relatively high salaries of professional employees that the division had assembled, overhead costs were high. In 1974, for the first time, the division reported a profit, but it was a relatively small percentage of sales. Sales volume continued to increase in 1975, and in that year a sizable profit was expected. Reported performance for the first six months of 1975 exceeded these expectations.

In July 1975 Brody, the financial vice president, received a letter from an accountant in the process systems division who had been recently discharged on grounds of incompetence. The ex-employee alleged that division management was furnishing false reports to corporate headquarters, giving many specific examples to back up his claims. Brody decided to have the matter looked into, and he sent a member of the internal audit staff to investigate. Within a week, the internal auditor reported that it was indeed likely that a serious problem existed, but that intensive work was required to measure its magnitude.

Brody immediately called in the public accountants and instructed them to perform a special audit of the division. He also reported the existence of the problem to the audit committee, and they in turn reported it to the board of directors. Throughout the investigation that followed, the board was kept fully informed.

By September, the investigation had uncovered the facts summarized below. The division had been audited by Tanner internal auditors in September 1974, in accordance with the regular audit program in which some divisions were assigned to outside auditors and others to internal auditors. That audit included an attempt to validate the inventory, but the cost accounting system was found to be so unreliable that it was not feasible to compare the book inventory with the physical inventory, even approximately. At that time, the internal auditors called attention to the system defects, acknowledging that these probably occurred because the cost accounting system had not kept up with the rapid growth of the division; they recommended improvements.

Sometime in 1974, control over the work-in-process inventory records had been lost. A job cost record was established for each component of every contract, but some material, parts and other costs of the component were not posted to this record. Consequently, the actual cost of the job was understated. When a component was billed to the customer, the job cost record was used as the basis for calculating the cost of goods sold, but because of the omitted items, cost of goods sold was understated and gross margin was correspondingly overstated. The total effect of correcting this error was to eliminate the division's reported profit for 1974 and to change the results for 1975 from an expected profit of $1 million to a loss of $1 million, on sales volume of $10 million.

After carefully examining the economics of the division, a team from corporate headquarters concluded that the prices negotiated for most existing contracts were too low. It also became clear that the advantages of the new process control system to the customer were not sufficiently great to permit prices to be increased enough to yield a satisfactory return on investment. Furthermore, investigation by a detective agency hired by the financial vice president indicated that the division manager was supporting a mistress and apparently living beyond his means. Nonetheless, adequate proof of illegal activities was never found. No other candidate for division manager was identified.

The division was closed after completing the backlog of contract work. During the phase-out period it was possible to reduce fixed costs so substantially that the eventual net loss on the whole operation was relatively insignificant.

Audit Committee Reactions. Members of the Audit Committee discussed the implications of this incident at length, both in formal meetings and informally. Dube and Spring were of the opinion that although there was clearly a breakdown in the control system, it was primarily attributable to the rapid growth in the activities of the process systems division. They pointed out that the failure to charge all costs to the job cost cards seemed to have started either shortly before or shortly after the 1974 audit. Since the practice was not prevalent at that time, it was unreasonable to expect the auditors to have detected it. They also pointed out that as soon as corporate management learned of the problem, it took prompt action and kept the audit committee and the board fully advised.

Hamel, the new member of the board, felt differently. He pointed out that the failure was a breakdown in the cost accounting system that corporate management didn't know about until an ex-employee spelled it out for them. Furthermore, he said, we can see with hindsight that the inventory reported by the division was growing at a suspiciously high rate. (Others replied that it was easy to see this by hindsight, but that at the time, the inventory growth was regarded as a commendable attempt to stockpile components and parts to fill the huge backlog of orders.) Although the final outcome in this case had practically no effect on profits, Hamel was concerned that there might be other more serious problems somewhere in the corporation that the committee had no inkling of, yet that the board was responsible for.

Hamel thereupon suggested to his colleagues that it might be a good idea to add the following sentence to the charter of the audit committee: "In carrying out its responsibilities, the audit committee may meet privately with the independent auditors, with internal auditors and with any employees, and may undertake such additional analyses as it deems necessary." His thought was that the audit committee would meet annually and privately with the manager of internal audit (who reported to the financial vice president), and that it would publicly encourage communication of relevant information from any corporate employee directly to the committee.

Spring was strongly opposed to this proposal, for three reasons. First, he said, the internal audit manager would not report anything to the audit committee that he had not already discussed with the financial vice president; if he did, he should be fired for disloyalty. Second, the very idea conveyed a distrust of management that was distasteful to him. Third, he envisioned the possibility that the audit committee would be deluged with crank letters that it was unequipped to handle. Dube tended to agree with Spring.

As of the end of 1975, Hamel's suggestion had been discussed only within the committee. Bentwood felt that if a formal proposal were made, it probably would be accepted by Remick and Brody, the president and financial vice president; to oppose such a proposal could be regarded as an implicit admission that there was something to hide. He also felt that their feelings would be hurt by such a proposal, and that it might lead to undesirable tension between management and the board. Based on years of contact, Bentwood had a high regard for both the ability and the integrity of Remick and Brody. He was, however, mindful of the new responsibilities that boards of directors were asked to assume, as well as the possibility of SEC or shareowner suits if at any time the board did not act with diligence.

Our Comment on Tanner Corporation

In retrospect, the system defect that precipitated the issue in this case seems obvious and should have been uncovered sooner. Either the division controller or the corporate controller should have been able to analyze the data and find out that profitability, as reported, was increasing at a rate that probably was higher than the facts warranted and/or that inventory was overstated. Moreover, only a few months previously, the internal auditor had explicitly stated that the cost accounting system was unreliable.

In reality, however, it is not surprising that the problem was not detected sooner. The financial statements reported good news—the division had shifted from a loss to a reported nice profit—and good news is not ordinarily scrutinized as carefully as bad news. The reported systems defects were probably judged to be a natural consequence of the rapid expansion of the division.

Although we think it is unrealistic to expect the audit committee to detect such problems before management does, the incident suggests that the committee might do well to scrutinize the statements more carefully. Questions from outside observers may suggest areas that management should look into, areas that may be overlooked in the pressure of day-to-day operations.

Hamel's proposal involves (1) scheduling private meetings with both the outside auditors and the internal auditors, and (2) encouraging employees to communicate directly with the audit committee.

The fact that the matter of private meetings with the auditors was controversial in 1975 indicates how things have changed since that time. Today, most audit committees meet privately with the auditors as a matter of course. The statement by Spring that an internal auditor should be fired if he doesn't discuss everything with the financial vice president is, in our opinion, only partly true. The internal auditor should discuss *most* things with his boss, but if he has reason to fear retribution, he is perfectly justified in going directly to the audit committee. The committee should protect him if he does so (and see that he gets fired if he does not).

The more important issue is whether the audit committee should encourage company employees (other than internal auditors) to report problems directly to it. The arguments, pro and con, are given in the case. In our view, the arguments against this practice are those of the old hands, and the arguments for it are typical of those made by newcomers to the committee. Newcomers feel their responsibility strongly and want all possible steps taken to ensure that problems come to their attention. They underestimate the practical problems inherent in an open-door policy. In part, these are the problems of dealing with a flood of personal gripes, most of which do not warrant the attention of directors. (The newcomer in this case actually received an employee's written complaint of a minor injustice, brought it up at an audit committee meeting, whereupon the committee spent time discussing it. We think the preferable course of action would have been to turn the complaint over to the controller without taking committee time, ask the controller to provide the basis for a response, and follow up to ensure that the matter had been looked into.)

More important than the potential workload problem is the likelihood of damaging relationships between the board and management. Management must manage, and managing includes dealing with personnel problems. Intrusion by the board can upset the lines of authority within the organization. The old hands on the committee recognize this, and being old hands ourselves we, of course, agree with them. The proposal involves meddling in management. To encourage everyone to have free acess to the audit committee would be a serious mistake.

At the same time, we recognize the need for vigilance. The committee cannot disregard problems that come to its attention, even though it has not requested that employees communicate such problems. In most cases, they will be personal gripes, but occasionally the whistle blower calls attention to a serious situation. From the symptoms described, the committee usually can judge whether the complaint is a personal gripe or a matter that is worth looking into. The Equity Funding case was one of the largest systems breakdowns ever, and there was a whistle blower; but the whistle blower could not get the attention of someone who was in a position to act until the situation had become disastrous.

One additional step might be warranted. The cost accounting system in the process system division was clearly defective. Was this an isolated case, or was it a symptom of a broader problem? One of us suggests that the audit committee should request a review of the systems in other divisions, particularly those with similar cost accounting systems, to ensure that the defect is not widespread. The other author believes that even this could be interpreted as an unwarranted intrusion on management's turf; he suggests that, at the most, the possibility should be raised informally with the financial vice president.

CASE
Hoover Corporation—Ethical Standards

In 1978 the directors of Hoover Corporation faced a difficult and delicate situation. Their problem concerned how they should deal with a fellow board member who was also the president and chief operating officer of the company, whose personal conduct became open to question.

Hoover Corporation was a large retail chain, with hundreds of retail outlets operating under the Hoover name, and a number of manufacturing divisions. In 1977 its sales were $4 billion, and aftertax profits were over $200 million. In recent years it had become a leading performer among retail chains. Within the industry, the company was regarded as being well managed, and it had the reputation of being aggressive but highly ethical in its practices. Hoover's securities were widely held; they usually traded at a modest premium over the securities of similar corporations.

Hoover's board included three insiders—the chairman and CEO, Byron Mortenson; the president and chief operating officer, Frank Leach; and the executive vice president of finance. The ten outsiders were people who were well regarded by the business community. Several were CEOs of major U.S. businesses—a New York City bank and a large auto manufacturer, for example—and there was also a retired senior government official and the president of a leading private university.

Outside board members frequently said that there was a family feeling among the Hoover board members and senior management that did not seem to exist with other boards—at least not to the same degree. Byron Mortenson, the chairman, made a special effort to encourage this feeling. For example, board meetings were occasionally held in different parts of the country where the company had operations; these occasions included pleasant social events, golf, and sightseeing, and spouses were invited to them. Such events enabled the participants to develop close friendships, without in any way sacrificing the serious work of the board.

Signs of Trouble.   During 1978 a series of events took place that were disturbing to the board and that posed particularly awkward problems for Richard O'Brien, chairman of the audit committee.

In February 1978 the corporate controller learned that during 1971 and 1972 corporate funds from Hoover's North Central Division apparently had been used to make political contributions. These contributions had been made from a secret fund that apparently had been created by cash transfers from several stores in the division. The amounts transferred were small, but they were improperly recorded as expenses on the books of the stores involved. Political contributions were made from the fund during 1971 and 1972, but the practice then ceased.

Federal law prohibits corporations from making political contributions. Moreover, having any kind of secret fund was in direct conflict with corporate policy. And, obviously, the falsification of accounting entries was a violation of accounting rules.

When the violation came to light, Byron Mortenson immediately informed the board, telling it that both the details and size of the transactions were still unclear. The board directed management to conduct a thorough investigation, to ascertain the facts and the persons involved in the 1971–1972 episode, and also to take steps to prevent a recurrence. The audit committee was designated to oversee this process.

The Investigation.   A prominent law firm, Phelps & Hamlin, was retained to advise and assist the company in conducting its investigation. The company's outside auditors were directed to determine how the secret fund had been created and specifically where the money came from.

As part of the investigation, Phelps & Hamlin prepared a detailed questionnaire, whose purpose was to elicit responses from members of corporate mangement concerning their knowledge of the existence of the secret fund and the disbursement of company funds for political purposes. This questionnaire covered the period 1971–1976 and required a signed response. It was sent to approximately 70 members of senior corporate management. The questionnaires were all returned directly to Phelps & Hamlin. That firm also interviewed in depth a number of members of corporate management.

The three corporate officers on the Hoover board were among those who filled out the questionnaire. The questionnaires that they submitted to Phelps & Hamlin indicated no involvement by them in the episode being investigated.

The investigation by Phelps & Hamlin and the accounting firm continued for several months, and many current and former employees were interviewed. The details of the transactions involved in creating the secret fund were gradually pieced together, as well as the amounts collected and disbursed. Although every penny could not be accounted for, both the lawyers and accountants agreed that the total amount was in the range of $40,000 to $50,000. It also seemed clear that these amounts were all disbursed as political contributions and that there was no direct benefit to any company employee. The lawyers and accountants concluded, however, that the collection and disbursement of this $40,000 to $50,000 could hardly have taken place without the knowledge, if not the direct participation, of the vice president in charge of the North Central Region, who in the early 1970s was Frank Leach, currently Hoover's president. Leach's written and signed response to the questionnaire stated that he had no knowledge of these transactions.

Board Considerations. The attorneys and accountants presented their findings, together with their evidence, to the audit committee and later to an executive session of the board, that is, a session in which only outside directors were present. The board decided to meet with Leach as soon as possible. The board directed the senior attorney of Phelps & Hamlin to meet privately with Leach prior to this meeting and present him with their evidence. They did so. A few days later the board in executive session met with Leach.

Leach was forthright, saying that he now recalled many of the events of 1971 and 1972 and that as well as he could recollect they were as indicated by the investigation. Not only did he remember the fund, but he also recalled participating in discussions about who would be the recipients of the contributions. He also acknowledged that as the senior executive in charge of the region, he was clearly the person responsible for this violation.

Richard O'Brien, chairman of the audit committee, had the uncomfortable task of chairing this meeting. He asked Leach why he had not reported the foregoing facts when he filled out and signed the questionnaire several months earlier. Leach said that in all honesty he had forgotten about the fund until the attorneys started presenting their findings to him. He pointed out that this had all happened six or seven years ago and that the amounts involved were small. Moreover, in those days there seemed to be a more permissive atmosphere regarding these matters. It was not uncommon for corporations to find "some way" to support or assist political candidates. He presented this not as an excuse for his indiscretion, but only as the reason why this episode had simply slipped his mind. He expressed deep regret over the incident and particularly for the embarrassment he was causing his fellow directors and corporate officers. He concluded by saying that he earnestly hoped that his involvement in something that had happened so long ago—and that involved a relatively small amount of money—would not impair his usefulness to the company.

After this meeting the attorneys advised the board that the company would have to file a Form 8-K with the SEC, presenting a full disclosure of the findings in this case. A copy of this report would be provided to each shareowner.

The directors pondered their next move.

All of the directors agreed that Leach was clearly the Number Two man in the company. Mortenson, the CEO, spent much of his time on external corporate affairs, and Leach was the leader so far as internal operating activities were concerned. He had an enormous amount of energy and charisma, was constantly traveling throughout the organization, and was well known and well liked. In fact, he probably knew more Hoover people personally than did Mortenson, and in many respects was closer to the organization. He had worked for Hoover ever since graduating from college and had always performed well in whatever task he was assigned. Not only was he a valuable corporate executive, but he probably had a closer and warmer personal relationship with the outside board members than any other corporate executive. It was generally considered that Leach was the leading candidate to succeed Mortenson.

Several directors emphasized that the amount involved was trivial in relation to Hoover's overall operations. Moreover, even though the episode violated both federal law and corporate policy, there really had been a more permissive attitude among corporations toward these matters in the early 1970s. They pointed to Watergate, beginning in 1973, as the event that had heightened sensitivity concerning corporate contributions, and they wondered if it was proper or necessary to apply current standards to events of an earlier time.

The directors could not ignore the fact that Leach had submitted a signed, falsified questionnaire in an inquiry initiated and directed by the board of directors, of which he was a member. This was, and would continue to be, a matter of record. Nevertheless, when confronted with the evidence, Leach had been totally forthcoming, he had acknowledged his involvement, and he had accepted full personal responsibility. Several board members said they believed that Leach was telling the truth, that they could understand how the incident could slip from his memory, and they expressed admiration for the way he had made a clean breast of the whole affair. They cautioned against overreaction by the board.

A number of directors expressed concern about how this

event—and especially how the board dealt with it—would be interpreted by Hoover's employees, customers, vendors, and the public at large. The Hoover board and management had always been proud of its reputation for high ethical standards. They believed that the company's record in this regard had been outstanding and that this was generally recognized and appreciated by employees, vendors, and customers. These directors felt that the board should do whatever was necessary to make it clear that Hoover's high standards would not be compromised.

In adjourning the meeting, O'Brien suggested that the board try to make up its mind on this case as soon as possible in fairness to all involved. The episode had already caused a considerable stir within the organization, and the matter would be exacerbated by the publication of the SEC Form 8-K. Any unnecessary delay would only make matters worse. He suggested that the alternatives ranged all the way from outright dismissal of Leach to some type of mild reprimand. He reminded the board that all the facts surrounding the incident, together with the board's action would be reported to the SEC and the shareowners.

Another meeting was scheduled for one week hence. O'Brien was unsure what his recommendation should be. He was, however, conscious of the fact that as chairman of the audit committee and one of the most senior directors, he would be looked to for leadership in bringing this matter to an appropriate conclusion.

Our Comment on Hoover Corporation

This is a case on the role that the board of directors plays in setting corporate standards. The money involved is insignificant; the standards aren't. The price is high.

The Hoover directors are between the proverbial rock and a hard place. They can allow Leach to remain with the company and wait for the affair to blow over. Or they can fire him, lose a key executive, but send a strong message on corporate standards. Either way they lose something and gain something. What is most important?

We are divided on this question.

One of us believes that on balance the mitigating circumstances warrant forgiveness. Standards regarding corporate political contributions certainly changed significantly between 1971 and 1978. When confronted, Leach withheld nothing. At least some of the directors thought he was telling the truth when he said he had simply forgotten his involvement six or seven years earlier. Neither he nor any other employee benefited from the contributions. The amount of money was trivial. Leach is an experienced, able executive—the backup for the CEO. He is also a friend and a fellow director. It would be overkill to dismiss him over this relatively minor incident. If he is retained, there might be an awkward but probably short period of adverse publicity, and perhaps some negative reaction. In a few months, however, almost everyone will have forgotten. The company would be back to business as usual, and the board would have retained one of its most valuable executives.

The other author believes that the arguments for dismissal are persuasive. Corporate standards start with the board of directors. If a board wants its company to have high standards in any area—product quality, employee performance, customer service, financial reporting or compliance with ethical and legal standards—the board itself must establish the standards and, equally important, it must constantly and consistently reinforce them by its own actions. The board's position, or the CEO's position backed by the board, on issues involving standards of corporate performance or corporate conduct, communicates strong messages to the entire organization.

The incident involving Leach is highly visible both inside and outside the Hoover Corporation. Moreover, whatever action is taken by the board will be reported to the SEC, and consequently to employees, shareowners, and the public at large. What message does the Hoover board want to send? If the board merely censures Leach and keeps him, the message is that Hoover's traditionally high standards of ethical and legal compliance have changed. The message conveyed is that it is no longer necessary to be so careful. It is now possible to get away with things. Maybe the board isn't so serious any longer about other standards, such as product quality, customer services, and who knows what. Another message is that if you are a big shot, especially a member of the board, the rules don't apply to you. It's only the little guy who gets hurt when he's caught. Is this the message the board wants to send?

The act of dismissing Leach would represent a strong reinforcement of the board's commitment to high standards of both ethical and legal compliance. The board's message is that it will fire even a fellow director and a valuable and popular executive rather than compromise its standards. Clearly this is an extremely powerful message to employees and to all other constituencies of Hoover Corporation. It demonstrates that this board really means business and that it insists that its standards in all areas of corporate life be taken seriously. Moreover, these standards will be applied consistently to everyone in the organization—from the top to the bottom. One author believes that this is the right message for the Hoover board to send, and to do so it has no alternative but to ask for Leach's resignation.

Our disagreement on this case is indicative of how people's judgments can differ. There is no right answer. The board did in fact ask for and receive Leach's resignation.

8

The Finance Committee

The board is responsible to the shareowners for monitoring the corporation's financial health and for assuring that its financial viability is maintained. Many boards have a finance committee that the board counts on to make recommendations on these matters. (Nonetheless, as emphasized in Chapter 7, the full board cannot escape its ultimate responsibility for sound decisions on these or other matters.)

The finance committee's agenda includes regular reviews of the corporation's financial condition and its financial policies; its long-and short-term financial requirements and how these requirements are to be met; dividends to be declared; and a review of capital and operating budgets. (If bonuses are determined in part by comparing actual performance against budget, the budget review also may be made by the compensation committee.)

In some companies the finance committee also reviews pension fund matters, including the policies that determine the annual contribution to the fund and the fund's investment performance. A separate pension review committee performs this function in other companies.

This chapter discusses how these functions are performed. While the existence of a finance committee is assumed here, it should be noted that in many corporations these functions are performed by the full board.

FINANCIAL POLICIES

Corporate financial matters are often complex and technical. They may encompass, for example, the specific terms of Eurobonds, variable rate bonds, and zero coupon bonds; interest rate swaps; employee stock ownership plans; leveraged buyouts; whether to hedge foreign exchange, and if so, how to do it; the use of factoring, lines of credit, certificates of deposit, and other credit instruments for short-term financing; policies regarding capital leases, and many others. Finance committee members cannot be expected to be knowledgeable about the intricacies of these matters—any more than they are expected to have the skills needed to evaluate a technically complex product design or production process.

The committee should, however, be concerned with the corporation's principal financial policies. It should try to ensure that these policies are consistent with one another and with the corporation's overall objectives. In doing so, the finance committee both monitors the company's financial condition and also judges management's ability to deal competently with the company's financial problems.

In a sense, a corporation is a financial machine. It obtains funds from various sources, it converts these funds to productive assets, and it uses these assets (together with its human resources) to produce outputs whose revenues are sufficient to provide a satisfactory return to those who supplied the funds. Two basic policies relating to this mechanism are the dividend payout policy and the debt policy. Other policies, such as those relating to stock splits and stock dividends, are much less important.

DIVIDEND POLICY

One of the board's responsibilities is to decide how much of the corporation's earnings should be distributed to the shareowners. Some companies regularly distribute a large fraction of earnings, while others retain most or all of the earnings in the corporation. Dividend policy and the quarterly dividend decision are especially important. Although generous dividends may be fine for the shareowner in the short run, such generosity can deprive the corporation of resources that are needed for growth and thereby penalize the shareowner in the long term. Conversely, if a large fraction of earnings is retained, shareowners may be deprived of the opportunity to make profitable alternative investments. Thus, the interest of both the corporation and its shareowners must be carefully weighed by the finance committee in making its recommendations to the board.

Some boards take a simplistic approach to dividends: "Always pay out x percent of earnings," or "Increase dividends each year, no matter what." Both of these statements have merit as rough guides in typical situations, but they are no more than that. In some industries a certain payout ratio is regarded as normal, and a company that departs markedly from industry practice may lose favor with investors. There is good evidence that a record of increasing dividends, or at least a record of stable dividends, is well regarded by investors. By contrast, an erratic dividend pattern is generally undesirable since it creates uncertainty for investors.

The dividend rate and any change in it also communicate to the investment community the board's attitude about the future. For example, in the first quarter of 1983, Boise Cascade declared its regular quarterly dividend of $47\frac{1}{2}$ cents per share, even though for the entire year ended December 31, 1982, the company had earned only 26 cents. This action was a clear signal of the board's confidence that earnings would recover, as indeed they did. By contrast, Caterpillar cut its dividend in 1983, a signal that its board believed that the company was faced with an extended period of depressed earnings, and that it was in the shareowners' best interests for the company to conserve its resources. This, likewise, turned out to be the case. In both instances the boards had difficult dicisions to make.

Dividend policy is clearly of such importance that it warrants careful analysis. The principal factors to be considered are:

- What are the company's financial needs? These needs depend on how fast the company wants to grow and how capable it is of growing. Or, as was the case with Caterpillar, what is needed to preserve the company during a period of adversity?
- How does the company want to finance its requirements for funds? It can meet its needs by retaining earnings, by issuing debt, by issuing equity, or by some combination. Each source of funds has its own cost and its own degree of risk.
- What return does the company expect to earn on shareowner equity, and what degree of risk is it willing to assume to achieve this objective? The trade-off between risk and return will determine the appropriate type of financing, and thus influence the extent to which earnings should be retained or paid out in dividends.

These are complex questions. Moreover, the factors involved in determining answers interact with one another. Hewlett-Packard is a useful example. When the company was organized in 1939, the founders decided to finance growth by reinvesting earnings. They thought the company could generate sufficient earnings to finance its growth, and they believed that this was the best investment they could make. Contributing to this decision was the obvious fact that as a "garage-in-the-backyard" startup, the company would have had to pay dearly for outside financing, with either debt or equity. This key decision established a dividend policy that continues today. Hewlett-Packard's growth has been financed from retained earnings; it has never issued equity, and it has only nominal debt. For many years the company paid no dividends at all, and in 1984 its payout was only about 10 percent of earnings. Hewlett-Packard shareowners are not interested in current dividends; they are looking for growth in the value of their shares. In 1983, Hewlett-Packard had revenues of $4.7 billion, aftertax income of $430 million, and stock with a market value of $10.5 billion.

AT&T is a successful company with quite different dividend and financing policies from those of Hewlett-Packard. AT&T has a long, unbroken record of stable dividends that are a relatively high percentage of earnings, normally at least $\frac{2}{3}$. Even in the depression years of the 1930s, the company maintained its regular dividends, although those dividends exceeded earnings in some periods. AT&T gained the reputation of being a widows' and orphans' stock—dependable dividends through thick and thin. The company's growth was financed by the issuance of both equity and debt.

These two examples indicate the extent to which dividend policy depends on an individual company's circumstances and needs. They also highlight the relationships between dividend policy, the company's need for financing, and the methods by which it chooses to meet its financial requirements. As we noted, these are not matters that lend themselves to simplistic solutions, and the finance committee should assure itself that management has an adequate rationale for its recommendations on dividends. An important basis for this assurance is the committee's judgment that the chief financial officer is competent.

Financial Reviews

Many finance committees (and often the entire board) are given an annual review of the company's financial policies in light of current performance, future plans, and perhaps changed external conditions. Such a meeting can benefit both the committee members and management. At the very least, the meeting provides discipline for the management group as they are forced to think through their position. Directors can raise questions that test the reasonableness of management's assumptions and the consistency of its policies.

When the dividend declaration is being considered, some companies present a multiyear forecast of the cash required to finance operations, the expected cash generation, anticipated financing, and the impact of dividends of various sizes. This gives the committee frequent opportunities to evaluate the appropriateness of the recommended dividend.

DEBT POLICY

The other important policy is the company's debt/equity ratio. This ratio is basically an expression of the company's attitude toward risk. Debt is inherently less expensive than equity, for two reasons. First, bondholders have greater assurance of receiving principal and interest payments than shareowners have of receiving dividends and earning capital gains, and investors therefore will furnish debt capital at a lower cost than they require for equity funds. Second (as of 1986 at least), debt interest is tax deductible to the corporation while dividends are not. If a company can be reasonably sure of meeting its debt service requirements and of earning a satisfactory ROI, each additional dollar of debt substituted for equity will earn an excess over its cost, and this excess accrues to the benefit of the shareowners.

But if a company *cannot* meet every one of its semiannual debt service requirements, it is in serious trouble. If leverage works, it is fine; if it doesn't work, bankruptcy looms. Thus, the basic trade-off is between the safety of a low debt/equity ratio and the risky possibility of a higher return with a high ratio, that is, with high leverage.

Investors pay attention to a company's debt/equity ratio, and they tend to regard the earnings of a company with a low ratio as having a somewhat higher quality than earnings of a similar company with a high ratio. The former company's securities may therefore trade at a higher P/E ratio than the latter.

Outside advisors can be helpful in establishing appropriate policies. Investment banks are constantly in touch with the financing markets and can give useful advice on the acceptable levels of debt, on the going rate of interest, on the probable reactions of credit rating agencies to a change in policy, and on the stock market's perception of the effect of such changes.

Nevertheless, the decision ultimately comes down to a gut feel of the appropriate balance between the riskiness of debt, and the greater safety inherent in equity financing. As the financial experts are fond of saying: "Management has to choose between sleeping well (i.e., with few worries about default on debt) and eating well (i.e., with the greater return produced by successful leverage)." It is obviously important that the board and management be in general agreement on the corporation's attitude toward risk.

Having decided on the appropriate balance between debt and equity, decisions on how to arrive at this balance are required if the current balance differs substantially from the desired norm. For example, if the corporation has too much equity, it can reduce the amount by increasing dividends, by obtaining additional capital by bonds rather than stock, or even by buying back some of its stock.

KEY RATIOS

A number of financial ratios are useful in evaluating financial performance. A regular review of these ratios is a relatively quick way for the finance committee to keep abreast of the corporation's financial condition. Some companies prepare a monthly report for the finance committee, covering the financial ratios that are important to them. A sample of such a report is shown

Table 1
Key Ratios

	Target 1984	August 1984	1983	1982	1981	1980
Working capital ($ in thousands)		891,114	742,965	394,872	534,252	494,948
Working capital turns	6.0	6.85	6.41	5.99	5.15	5.62
Inventory turnover	4.0	4.1	3.6	2.4	3.2	3.4
Receivables, days sales	52	53.3	51.6	52.4	52.3	54.2
Total debt ($ in thousands)		447,203	447,712	425,253	596,696	597,122
Debt/debt plus equity	30%	26.2%	29.0%	33.3%	35.1%	35.2%
Interest coverage	5	7.19	2.82	(.47)	3.46	2.96
Cash coverage, fixed charges	6	9.59	5.22	(.44)	4.75	4.20
Dividends paid/EPS	20%	18.1%	26.1%	(67.7%)	36.8%	40.5%
Tangible assets/funded debt	250%	346.8%	315.2%	285.6%	269.9%	276.5%

in Table 1. Other companies will find different information useful.

INVESTOR RELATIONS

Although there are millions of shareowners in the United States, most decisions to buy or sell securities are based on the recommendations of a few thousand financial analysts. These analysts influence the actions of investment firms directly, and they influence individual shareowners through market letters or other forms of advice. The number of analysts who follow a given company regularly is rarely more than two dozen, and for most companies, it may be only a dozen. The CEO and other senior managers typically go to great lengths to keep the company's regular analysts well informed and to answer requests from others who may be interested.

Analysts want all the information they can get, including the opinions of the company's directors. How should directors respond to questions from them and from other interested individuals? We suggest that directors should be extremely circumspect. For one thing, they are vulnerable to both civil and criminal penalties if they violate the rules about the improper use of inside information. More important, the company should speak with a single voice, and that should be the voice of the CEO or his designate. If, by words or facial expressions, a director conveys either a more optimistic or a more pessimistic view than the CEO's about the company's prospects, the analyst is uncertain whom to believe. If the director provides information not revealed by the CEO, the analyst's confidence in the CEO's frankness is shaken. Although analysts may press a director in the hope of obtaining a nugget of information, most analysts are well aware of the principle that only the CEO or his designate should speak for the company. In fact, those who ask the questions actually do not expect astute directors to be forthcoming. The most they hope for is that they might catch a director off guard.

The same principle should govern a director's contact with reporters.

PENSIONS

The finance committee considers two aspects of pension fund policy: (1) the amount required to be added to the fund and (2) the investment of the fund. As is the case with other financial issues, policies result from a mixture of sound analysis and personal attitudes toward risk.

Size of the Pension Fund

Most corporate pension plans are defined benefit plans. In deciding on the size of the fund required to make benefit payments to retirees, directors tend to rely heavily on the opinion of an actuary. Given facts about the size and demographic characteristics of the covered employees, facts about the provisions of the plan, and assumptions about the return on investment of the fund and about probable wage and salary increases over time, an actuary can calculate the size of the pension fund that is currently needed to meet these future requirements. (With available computer software, the company can make the same calculations.)

However, there is no way of knowing the reasonableness of the two key assumptions: the future return on investment, and the future wage and salary payments that will be the basis for the amount of the pension payments. Since the actuarial calculations are no more valid than the accuracy of these assumptions, the calculations should not be taken as gospel. Both of these variables are roughly related to the future rate of inflation, and the spread between them should remain roughly constant. When one of these variables is changed, it is likely that there should be a corresponding change in the other; that is, an increase of one percentage point in the assumed return on investment should probably be accompanied by a corresponding increase in the assumption about compensation.

Pension Fund Investments

The most conservative practice is to invest the pension fund in annuities or in bonds whose maturities match the anticipated pension payments. Such a policy is said to lock in the ability to make payments. With respect to pensions of employees who have already retired, this is so. It is not necessarily so, however, for employees who are currently working. If their compensation increases at a faster rate than is assumed in the actuarial calculation or if the plan itself is sweetened, the fixed return will turn out to be inadequate. Under a defined benefit plan, there is no sure way of guaranteeing that the cash will be available when it is needed. In any event, with such a conservative policy the company gives up the opportunity of earning the sometimes greater return from an investment in equities.

Most companies hire one or more banks or investment firms to manage the pension fund. Voluminous data are available on the past performance of such managers. The catch is, however, that an excellent past record is no guarantee of excellent future performance. Any firm is a collection of individuals. Investment performance is partly a function of the individual doing the investing, and the record can change when the individual leaves or loses his skill. Performance is also partly a matter of luck.

Some companies divide the fund among several managers, periodically compare their performance, and replace the one with the poorest record. This may spread the risk somewhat, but it does not guarantee optimum performance; luck and the ability of the individuals concerned continue to be dominant factors.

Although judging performance is difficult, it is a fact that some managers are better than others. The finance committee therefore watches performance carefully, is cautious about making changes as a result of short-run aberrations, but prompt to do so when it is convinced that a better manager has been identified.

The finance committee also decides on the broad investment policies: how much in equities, how much in fixed income securities, how much in real property, how much in new ventures, how much in overseas securities, the maximum in a single company or industry, and so on.

CONCLUSION

Tools of analysis are available and have become more useful with the advent of the computer. Management, not the finance committee, is responsible for using analytical tools for evaluating risk. These tools help quantify the risk, but they are not a substitute for a definite policy on risk. An attitude toward risk is a personal feeling, and the finance committee should recognize it as such. Each CEO has a personal attitude toward risk, as do individual directors.

The board's responsibility is to probe management's rationale for its policies and thereby assure itself that management has thought them through and that the policies are within acceptable limits. If the above criteria are met, then the policies should be accepted by the finance committee and the board.

CASE
Grady Company—A Maverick Director

In 1983, following a series of what he considered to be rebuffs by his fellow Grady Company directors, Warren Judge was so frustrated that he was considering resigning from the board.

Background. Grady Company manufactured several lines of hardware and sold them through its own retail stores, through hardware chains, mail order catalog houses, and independent hardware retailers. Its history went back over 100 years. Until 1950 the company was owned and managed by one family. In 1950 it went public and was listed on the New York Stock Exchange. Descendants of the funding family continued to be dominant in management and were well represented on the board of directors.

In 1973, the company fell on hard times, principally because of the unsettled economic conditions associated with the OPEC oil embargo. It was unable to maintain the ratios specified in its bond indentures and therefore faced a financial crisis. At the urging of the board, the CEO and two other family board members resigned. The new CEO, Philip Meyers, had been president of the division that operated Grady's retail stores. He had 20 years of service with Grady, with experience principally in marketing, and had been a director since 1969.

Meyers did a remarkable job of turning the company around. Restructured financial arrangements were worked out with banks, ending the financial crisis. Dividends, which had been discontinued in 1973, were resumed in 1975. The company became profitable in 1974, with each subsequent year's income thereafter setting a new record. In 1983, revenue was $910 million, and net income was $82 million.

One of the family members who resigned in 1973 had been the financial vice president. Meyers replaced him with Fred Jennings, who had been controller of another company and who had no previous experience in the hardware business. As family directors reached retirement age, they were replaced with outsiders who had no connection with the family or the company.

Warren Judge was one of the new directors. He was a professor of finance at a leading business school, and he taught in an executive development program that Meyers had attended. Meyers was impressed by Judge's knowledge of finance, his ability, and his outgoing personality. Judge was already a director of a large, highly respected stockbrokerage firm. The managing director of that firm, a friend of Meyers, gave Judge a glowing recommendation. Meyers asked the board to consider Judge as a director, and he invited Judge to attend informal gatherings held in connection with the next two board meetings so that board members would have an opportunity to get to know him. Several directors were enthusiastic about Judge, and none expressed reservations. He was elected a director in February 1978, and reconfirmed at the annual shareowners meeting in May 1978.

Meyers assigned Judge to the finance committee of the board. This committee met quarterly to recommend dividends, and to take up other financial questions. Meyers sometimes attended, but management was usually represented by the financial vice president, Fred Jennings.

Dividend Policy. At the first two meetings of the finance committee, the only subject discussed was dividends. No change in the dividend rate was proposed. Judge kept quiet at these meetings; he believed that a new committee member should not say much until he had become thoroughly familiar with the personalities and the issues.

During the meeting at which the first quarterly dividend for 1979 was considered, Jennings proposed an increase to $0.35 a share, that is, $1.40 per share on an annual basis. Earnings in 1978 had been $4.80 a share, and annual dividends had been $1.20 a share for the past two years. Jennings reasoned that the current rate was only a 33 percent payout of earnings and the proposal would increase the rate to 37 percent. He said that the usual practice in the industry was a payout ratio of 40 percent. Initially, there was no discussion of this proposal. After a pause, Judge asked whether an analysis of future cash flows had been made; this should show whether enough cash would be available to meet working capital and other needs after the larger payout. Jennings said that although no such analysis had been made, he was comfortable with the financial picture. Judge said no more and voted for the increase.

After the meeting, Judge talked informally with Jennings about dividend policy. Judge said that he did not believe there was such a thing as a *right* payout ratio, and he hoped that future dividend proposals would be accompanied by a thorough analysis of the company's financial requirements and how they were to be met. Thereafter, Jennings presented a cash flow analysis to the committee each time a dividend increase was proposed. Other members paid little attention to it, however.

Stock Split. In a meeting in 1981, Jennings proposed that the stock be split, two for one. He said that the stock was currently selling for about $60 a share, and he believed that any price above $50 a share tended to reduce its attractiveness, especially to small investors. (In 1973, the stock had traded at $6 a share.) Judge knew of several academic studies which showed that low-priced stocks were generally neither more nor less attractive than high-priced stocks. He made this point at the meeting, although he could not recall at the time the specifics of these studies. Judge also pointed out that more than half of Grady stock was now owned by institutions, and he doubted that a low price affected their attitude toward Grady.

Other committee members were not convinced by these points, nor was Jennings. The committee voted unanimously for the stock split, and the board ratified its recommendation. Judge did not comment on this topic at the meeting of the full board.

Bond Call. In 1982, Jennings proposed that the company's $40 million outstanding bond issue be called. Meyers was present at this meeting and strongly supported the recommendation. Jennings pointed out that Grady Company had the necessary funds, and that getting rid of the bond issue would greatly lessen the possibility of a financial crisis such as the one that had occurred in 1973. He presented a one-page set of numbers which indicated that operations would generate enough cash to meet working capital needs, even after paying out the $40 million. Additional funds would be necessary for expansion, but these could be obtained by factoring receivables or by leases, rather than by borrowing.

Judge was dismayed by this analysis. He thought that the estimate of financial needs was extremely superficial, that no consideration had been given to the advantages of leverage, that the factoring and leasing alternatives were not addressed in depth, and that in general the directors were not given adequate information as a basis for such a significant decision. Judge expressed these opinions, adding that directors should have been given an analysis prior to the meeting for an issue that was so important.

No other director supported him. Judge cast the sole vote against the recommendation in committee, spoke up against it in the board meeting, and cast the sole negative vote at that meeting. He sensed that other directors were unhappy about his action, characterizing it as a vote of no confidence in management, especially Jennings.

Inventory Policy.   Grady Company costed its inventory on a first-in, first-out (FIFO) basis. About half the other public companies in its industry used the last-in, first-out (LIFO) basis. In periods of inflation, the LIFO basis results in higher cost of sales and hence in lower taxable income. However, it also results in lower reported earnings because a company that uses LIFO for income tax purposes must also use the LIFO method in reporting its income to shareowners. (At the time, this was the only important situation in which a company had to use the same method in its financial statements that it used in calculating its taxable income.)

Ever since joining the board, Judge had doubted the wisdom of the company's inventory costing policy. In a discussion with Jennings in 1979, he had suggested that switching to LIFO would be advantageous, but he had received no encouragement. In 1981, the income tax regulations were changed; thereafter, although companies on a LIFO basis for tax purposes had to report income calculated on that basis, they could include information in the notes to the financial statements that made it easy to calculate what income was on the FIFO basis. Judge felt that this removed the principal obstacle to the adoption of LIFO. He discussed this at length with Jennings, but still received no support.

In 1983 Judge prepared an analysis which showed that on the LIFO basis the company should generate $90 million of additional cash over the next ten years from reduced income taxes, and that by the tenth year the reinvestment of this cash should make reported earnings, even under LIFO, almost equal to what they would be under FIFO. He asked that the LIFO topic be put on the Board's agenda, and this was done.

At a joint meeting of the finance and audit committees, the proposal was discussed. Management continued to oppose it, stating that stock market analysts tended to disregard the effect of LIFO and to look primarily at the number reported as earnings. Jennings told the committees of conversations he had had with several analysts that confirmed this assertion. Judge cited studies which showed that although a shift to LIFO depressed stock prices initially, the effect lasted for only about a year.

Of the seven board members present at the joint meeting, only three voted for the proposal. At the full board meeting, the same three voted for LIFO, but there were nine votes against it.

Judge's Reaction.   Judge was discouraged by this vote. Looking back over his five years of service on the board, he could see that on most financial issues he was out of step with management and with the majority of board members. He did not blame Meyers, the CEO, because he felt that Meyers was not an expert in finance and relied heavily on Jennings. He did not particularly blame his fellow directors, because they, too, relied on Jennings. He was convinced that Jennings had the confidence of stock market analysts who followed Grady Company. He wondered whether the best course of action might be not to stand for reelection in 1984. The Grady assignment had not turned out to be fun.

Our Comment on Grady Company Case

Finance is an esoteric subject. Although great progress has been made in recent years in validating certain propositions about the behavior of stock prices, the most important decisions continue to be based largely on judgment. Moreover, finance is a rapidly changing field. Board members cannot be expected to keep up with developments unless they do so in connection with their principal occupation. Most must rely on the opinions of others, and they naturally turn to the company's chief financial officer for advice.

Grady's management and directors seemed to be influenced heavily by the financial crisis of 1973. This appropriately made them cautious. However, the proposal to retire bonds and give up the advantages of leverage may have been unduly cautious. There is no indication that alternatives were studied, such as the possibility of using excess cash to acquire Grady Company stock, rather than calling the bond issue. Management and directors also seemed to be guided by rules of thumb (e.g., a payout ratio of 40 percent) rather than by the careful analysis that many companies undertake.

Judge is a professor. There is a widespread feeling that professors are out of touch with the real world and that their theories are unrealistic. This opinion is, in many cases, warranted. Judge, however, does not appear to be in this category. He is a board member of a respected financial house and is well regarded by its management. Nevertheless, he may feel that Grady Company management is not really convinced of his qualifications, and that since board members usually support management, he is accomplishing very little.

On the other hand, although Judge is an expert on finance, it doesn't necessarily follow that he is always right and that everyone should defer to his views. There is now, and always will be, a great deal of judgment involved in financial decisions. Thus, although Judge's opinions appear to be quite sound, he should nevertheless respect the views of his fellow directors, even though he disagrees with them.

Above all else, he should recognize that he performs an important role on the finance committee and the board by raising questions and initiating discussion of issues that otherwise probably never would be considered. That his position on the LIFO matter received some support from other board members indicates that he may gradually be exerting more influence than he thinks. Judge has put forth his ideas in what seems to us to be a reasonable fashion. He did not speak up at the early meetings because he was unsure of the environment. Later, he presented his ideas initially to management, rather than raising them at committee meetings without prior notice. He disagreed publicly with management only when he was not given advance notice of an issue or when he had failed to convince management of the soundness of his views.

His advocacy of LIFO has now divided the board, and probably has shaken the confidence of at least two of its members in the ability of the financial vice president. Should he end this divisiveness by resigning from the board?

We believe that either course of action—resigning or staying—can be supported. However, if he resigns, it should be for purely personal reasons—board membership is no longer a satisfying experience. He should not resign simply because he finds himself differing with some of his fellow directors on a few matters. A board should have a variety of viewpoints, and there should be a wide-ranging discussion of important issues. And in such a discussion, not everyone can win all the time. Judge performs a useful role and makes a positive contribution. The board is better because he is on it.

If Judge stays, he can continue his advocacy of policies that he believes are in the best interests of the shareowners, a real-world situation that is probably more exciting than the classroom. Although he is depressed after his defeat on the LIFO matter, he may soon conclude that the challenge of continuing to work for what he believes to be right will be rewarding once more.

We hope he decided to stay.

Star and Moon—Pension Fund Issues

Don Arnold, retired CEO of a medium-size manufacturing company, was an outside board member of two companies that had taken diametrically opposite positions on a pension fund matter. He didn't see how both companies could be right.

Star Products, Inc.   At the March 1984 meeting of the finance committee of Star Products, Inc., Kevin Mallen, its chief financial officer, proposed that in order to meet its pension obligation for employees who had already retired, the company should fund this obligation with bonds whose maturities would be scheduled so as to meet payout requirements of the retiree group. Arnold thought this was a fine idea and enthusiastically endorsed management's plan.

Star's pension fund totaled more than $340 million, and the vested benefits under the company's pension plans were over 90 percent funded. The plans' earnings assumption was 8 percent, and the assumption for wage and salary increases was 6 percent. Over the past five years the fund had earned, on the average, over 12 percent annually. The finance committee was comfortable with the status of the plan and was pleased with its investment performance.

Mallen proposed that $75 million of the pension fund be set aside and invested in bonds to meet the pension obligation of retirees. He reasoned that the amount of the obligation to retirees was calculated within close limits on an actuarial basis, and that bonds could be purchased now with an average yield of over 13 percent to meet this obligation. Moreover, maturities could be arranged to coincide with payment schedules, so that there would be no further risk with respect to this portion of Star's pension obligation. The balance of the fund ($340 million less the $75 million) would be favorably affected. The total fund (before deducting the $75 million), on the basis of the 8 percent earnings assumption, included almost $100 million that was held or earmarked to meet the retirees' pension obligation. By funding this obligation with $75 million of bonds at 13 percent, the remaining fund would immediately cover over 100 percent of vested obligations. Consequently, future company payments to fund the pension plan for active employees would be significantly reduced.

Arnold and the other directors viewed this proposal as a no-lose deal and urged Mallen to implement it as soon as possible. The finance committee reported its recommendation to the full board, which voted unanimously to proceed.

Moon Company. A few weeks later, Arnold attended a meeting of another board, Moon Company. At an informal dinner of directors and senior management the night before the meeting, Arnold described the action recently taken by Star Products to Moon's senior financial officer, Al Werolin, and several outside directors. The Moon and Star situations were similar, and Arnold suggested that Moon proceed now with such a plan while bond yields were so high.

Arnold was greatly surprised at the negative response to his suggestion. Werolin said that he and his staff had looked into this type of plan, but they considered it unwise and had decided not to recommend it to the Moon board. His basic reasoning was that he was reluctant to commit so much of the company's pension fund to fixed income securities as contrasted with equities. He believed that five to ten years in the future there was a very good chance that equities would produce returns well in excess of bonds—even at their current high yields. If this turned out to be the case, the company's pension expense would be lower than under Arnold's proposal. Werolin also pointed out that in the last several years the performance of Moon's pension fund had improved significantly (it still did not quite equal Star's performance level, however), and he was generally quite optimistic about the future for equities. Two of the three other outside directors who participated in this informal discussion tended to agree with Werolin.

Arnold wondered who was right.

Our Comment on Star and Moon

The different positions of Star and Moon in this case reflect a basic difference in attitudes. This difference affects many more issues than just the policy of pension-fund investments. It lies behind an individual director's opinion on dividend policy, the debt/equity ratio, and most other financial issues. It is the basic reason, although often unstated, for opinions on many other matters. Essentially, the difference stems from a philosophical difference in individual attitudes toward risk.

Some people believe that risk should be minimized. They accept only the degree of risk that is judged to be necessary to earn a satisfactory return on investment. They oppose policies that are estimated to produce a more profitable outcome but that involve greater risk. They regard such policies as unwarranted speculation, as being inconsistent with the directors' fiduciary responsibility, even as gambling with the company's funds. In this case, the desired result of assuring that retired employees will receive their pension payments can be achieved by the low-risk policy of investing in bonds that mature when the pension payments are due.

Other people are willing to take more risk if they are convinced that there is a good chance of earning a higher return. They believe that their duty is to earn the highest return that can reasonably be achieved. In this case, they favor investment in a portfolio that contains some equities, because they believe there is an excellent chance of earning a higher return on such a portfolio than through investing solely in bonds, and that the company's ultimate contribution to the pension fund will therefore be lower than with the safer alternative. They recognize, and accept, the risk that such a policy may not work out.

The point of this is *not* that one of these approaches is right and the other is wrong. Indeed, one of us favors the Star approach while the other agrees with Moon. Rather, the point is that directors should recognize that their colleagues have this basic difference in attitude, and that they have it in varying degrees. It is highly unlikely that arguments, however rational they may be, will cause a director to change his approach.

Failure to appreciate this point can result in fruitless acrimony. Reconciling such philosophical differences is one of the crucially important tasks of the effective director.

9

Nonprofit Organizations

$\mathbf{B}$oards of directors (often called trustees) of nonprofit organizations come in all sizes and shapes.

At one extreme, there is the board that performs many of the functions that the CEO performs in the typical business. The organization has a manager (often called executive director) who corresponds to the chief operating officer of a business, but the board makes all the policy decisions. Fraternal organizations, country clubs, condominium associations, and some churches are examples of such organizations.

At the other extreme, the board is normally not a decision-making body; it makes decisions only in times of crisis. In some of these organizations, the managing director is the undisputed boss who makes both policy and operating decisions. He is the driving force behind the organization, often its founder. Project Hope, CARE, and RIF, as well as many local social service organizations, are examples. In museums, orchestras, ballet companies and similar arts organizations, there is an artistic director, who in many cases ranks as high as, or nearly as high as, the managing director. The members of the board of such organizations select the managing director and perhaps the artistic director, raise money, keep the managing director and artistic director in touch with the community, and lend their prestige to

193

the organization. Many of them support its activities with substantial commitments of time and money.

Between these extremes is the type of board we shall focus on in this chapter. It is in many respects similar to the board of a business. Like a business board, its basic function is to ensure that the policies and the management are such that the organization will continue to be a successful, viable institution. Boards of hospitals, colleges and universities, and research organizations are examples. Differences between such a board and the board of a profit-oriented company in the same industry (such as SRI International vs. Arthur D. Little, Inc.) may not be substantial. Nevertheless, most of these boards do differ from those of businesses in some important respects.

DIFFERENCES BETWEEN NONPROFIT ORGANIZATIONS AND BUSINESSES

Authority of the Chief Executive Officer

In any well managed organization the CEO is Number One, the organization's leader. In the typical nonprofit organization, the nature of the leadership role differs from that in the typical business in ways that affect the functioning of the board.

The chairman of the board of most business corporations is either the CEO or another full time employee. With rare exceptions, the chairman of the board of a nonprofit organization is not an employee and is associated with the organization only on a part-time basis. His responsibilities are different from those of a CEO, and this creates a different set of relationships between the board and the chief executive officer.

Moreover, especially in organizations staffed with professionals, the CEO's authority may be less than that of the CEO in a business. The CEO (president, general manager, managing director) of a symphony orchestra, a ballet, an opera company, or other arts organization, may have only slightly more authority than the conductor, the choreographer, the musical director, or the star performer. The CEO of a hospital may in fact have less real authority than the chief of the medical staff. Clark Kerr, distinguished educator and president of the University of California said:

> The president of a multiversity is leader, educator, wielder of power, pump; he is also officeholder, caretaker, inheritor, consensus seeker, persuader, bottleneck. But he is mostly a mediator.

The CEO of a nonprofit organization tends to have less general management experience than the CEO of a business. The CEO of a university may be known as an outstanding educator, the CEO of a research laboratory as an outstanding scientist, but neither may be known as an outstanding manager. In the last few decades, there has been an increasing recognition of the importance of a CEO's ability to manage, however.

Diversity in Board Members' Background

Although they may not be familiar with the company's industry, most members of a business board are familiar with business—its vocabulary, the approach to analyzing problems, sources of funds, the budgeting process, and so on. Some members of nonprofit boards have no business background, and thus lack a common starting point for dealing with businesslike problems. Conversely, the members of the board who are businessmen usually are unfamiliar with the unique characteristics of nonprofit organizations: academic freedom in a university, the dominance of physicians in a health care organization, reluctance to accept authority in a research organization, artistic temperament in an arts organization.

Less Commitment by Board Members

Members of business boards are paid—usually less per hour than they could earn elsewhere, but nevertheless more than a trivial amount. Members of nonprofit boards not only are unpaid, but they are expected to contribute substantial amounts of money if they have the means. Perhaps for this reason, nonprofit board members typically do not have as strong a commitment as business board members. They do not do as much homework; they do not feel as strong an obligation to attend meetings. (There are, of course, dedicated board members who devote substantial time to the institution, but they are exceptions.)

More Functions Performed by the Board

In many nonprofit organizations, especially small ones, important functions are performed by board members as volunteers. Often, the treasurer is a bank official or accountant, who either supervises the organization's accountant or even does the bookkeeping and cash handling personally. A volunteer lawyer may perform the functions of in-house counsel. A skilled fund raiser or an expert in the related fields of advertising or public relations is a treasure. So is the politician who can lower barriers and suggest a path that leads to smoother relationships with government agencies. In return for these services, the volunteer expert has the prestige and fellowship associated with board membership. Some may also obtain valuable professional contacts from this association.

In most organizations with endowments, a committee of the board sets endowment policy, has a large say in the selection of endowment managers, and appraises the performance of the endowment manager. In some business organizations a board committee performs these functions for the pension fund, but usually the committee merely ratifies management's recommendations.

Unwieldy Size

Nonprofit boards tend to be large, far above the optimum size for effective decision making at meetings of the full board. For this reason, full board meetings tend to be held less frequently than in businesses, and most of the important deliberations take place in committees.

Difficulty of Measuring Performance

Although not by any means the only criterion, profitability—the bottom line—provides a useful first approximation in assessing the current performance of a profit-oriented corporation. There is no analogous measure of performance for a nonprofit organization. A deficit does indicate trouble, but a large black number on the bottom line of the income statement does not reveal anything important about how well the organization has performed. A nonprofit organization is judged primarily by the quality of the work it does. Extremely good or extremely poor performance may be easily detected, but when an organization falls within these extremes, it is difficult to judge its improvement or deterioration.

COMPOSITION OF THE BOARD

The general rule is that there are three qualifications to sit as a director of a nonprofit organization—Wealth, Work, and Wisdom—and that each board member should have at least two of these. This suggests that wealth alone is not enough; the wealthy member should actively participate by getting others to support the organization. Work alone is not enough; the hard-working, dedicated, but inept person can disrupt the normal functioning of meetings (but the hard-working, wealthy person is welcome, even if inept). Wisdom alone is not enough; there is rarely room for the lazy sage.

These qualifications are of course gross simplifications. They do suggest that, contrary to what many people believe, the board of a nonprofit organization needs members who will work hard for the organization and whose judgment is sound, even if their financial resources are modest.

Financial Supporters

Some people are invited to become members because they are wealthy, because they have access to wealth, or both. In return, these donors have the satisfaction of participating in an endeavor in which they strongly believe, and, within limits, they can shape the program of the organization. Since their support may be crucial to the organization's financial health, and their withdrawal because of disenchantment with the program may be catastrophic, their views are given more than ordinary weight. Good supporters recognize this fact. They are careful not to throw their weight around unduly, or to push for a pet project that is peripheral to, or even inconsistent with, the organization's objectives. (They have a right to a pet project that is not outright harmful, if they finance it with an incremental contribution.)

In general, but with many exceptions, the need for wealthy board members is less now than it was two or three decades ago. Foundations now provide much of the financial support for which the wealthy individual was formerly the direct source. Patients provide most of the revenues of health care organizations, either directly or through insurance companies, the government and other third parties. The United Way channels the community's funds to social service and other local organizations. Many government agencies support education and research through grants and contracts. The board member who is knowledgeable about these sources may be more important to the organization than the individual who has personal wealth.

Clients and Employee Members

Beginning in the 1960s there was pressure to add clients and/or employees to many boards: students and faculty members to university boards, welfare recipients and other clients to social service agency boards. The performance of such board members, however, has not been entirely satisfactory. Even though they have the best intentions, they tend to focus on short-run solutions, without regard to their long-run implications. Also, perhaps subconsciously, they tend to advocate policies that are in their self interest or the interest of their constituents, rather than thinking of the best interests of the entire organization. Some make speeches, often long-winded and threatening, that impede the process of sound decision making.

A related manifestation of the same tendency has been the passage of sunshine laws in the federal government and many states. These laws require that the general public be admitted to board meetings of government and government-sponsored organizations, even to such highly sensitive committee meetings as those involving the selection of a new CEO or the evaluation of a current CEO. However, the undesirable consequences of sunshine laws seem to be increasingly recognized, and the peak of this movement seems to have passed. There is currently a tendency to have clients represented by people who attend board meetings and participate in the discussion, but who do not vote.

Should physicians be on hospital boards? Unlike many other types of special-interest representatives, they are well informed, mature, and often base their judgments on what they believe to be in the long-run interest of the hospital. They, rather than the patients, are the real constituents of the hospital. Thus, our reservations about special-interest representation do not apply as strongly to hospital boards.

Minorities

The problem of getting female, black, Hispanic, and other minority representation on the boards of nonprofit organizations is essentially the same as the problem for business organizations, discussed in Chapter 4. Such representatives should be sought, but not to the point of inviting unqualified persons.

Effect on Decision Making

As we pointed out in Chapter 5, a board with more than about 18 members is unwieldy. It must depend on committees to analyze most of the issues and to make recommendations; these are then discussed and usually accepted by the full board. Selecting members from the various categories outlined above tends to lead to large boards. The members of such boards must recognize that decision making must then be left largely to committees; they must also discipline themselves to take only their fair share of the available time in discussions at board meetings.

RELATIONSHIP TO THE CHIEF EXECUTIVE OFFICER

Several considerations complicate relationships between the chairman of the board and the CEO.

- The board chairman is usually not an employee.
- The board carries out some functions that are carried out by the CEO in a business organization.
- Authority within the organization may be divided between the CEO and professionals.
- Influential board members must be kept happy.

These considerations suggest special relationships between the chairman of the board and the CEO. The chairman is (1) a buffer, (2) a confidant, and (3) in some circumstances, a mediator.

Buffer

Within limits, the chairman acts as a buffer between the board and management, both the CEO and other executives. He lets board members know that they are expected to discuss important complaints, requests, and ideas first with him, rather than going to the CEO or others in the organization. In particular, board members should not give direct advice to professionals—faculty members in a college, physicians in a hospital, social workers in a welfare agency, and, above all else, artists in an arts organization.

This does not mean that all communications between board members are funneled through the chairman to the CEO. There is an understanding that certain individual requests are properly directed at others in the organization: parking privileges, tickets to events, inquiries about admissions to a college, and the like. Also, the chairmen of board committees deal directly with their counterparts in the organization on many matters. Nevertheless, the chairman sees to it that board members do not act behind the CEO's back on matters that the CEO wants to be aware of. And, of course, the chairman does not himself go around the CEO.

The chairman also acts as a buffer between the CEO and external parties, although his abililty to do this is more limited than his ability to rein in board members. Inevitably, the CEO is the lightning rod that attracts outside criticism. The chairman can, however, intervene in important cases and perhaps lower the voltage. Legally, the board, not the CEO, has ultimate responsibility for the organization. The chairman can use this fact to draw fire away from the CEO in certain circumstances: threat of a discrimination suit, trouble stirred up by a disgruntled employee, and the like.

Confidant

Ideally, the chairman and the CEO have a good personal relationship. The CEO feels comfortable confiding his concerns about people and policies to the chairman. Even if the chairman does no more than listen sympathetically, the therapeutic value can be great. Sometimes the chairman, as an outside observer, can suggest solutions that may not have occurred to the CEO.

The CEO tries out new ideas on the chairman in private, and the chairman discusses his new ideas, or those of other board members, to the CEO before they are aired publicly. From whichever direction an idea emanates, it rarely is pushed further unless both the chairman and the CEO agree that it is worth pursuing.

The chairman tends to have a longer-range perspective than does the CEO. Much of the CEO's time is occupied with current problems. In their informal discussions, therefore, the chairman may focus more attention on long-range plans than would otherwise be the case.

Mediator

When an organization has two leaders, an official chief executive officer and a leader of the professional group (e.g., physician, scientist, professor, artist), a difference of opinion between the two can have serious consequences. In 1984, a well-publicized dispute erupted between the CEO of the San Francisco Ballet and its choreographer. Each was supported by a faction of the board. The chairman, Neil Harlan, spent much time and energy working on the problem, notwithstanding his full time job as CEO of a multibillion-dollar company. Although the chairman can sometimes mediate these disputes, the personalities of the two parties are likely to be so different that mediation is extraordinarily difficult. Fortunately, this problem does not arise frequently.

RELATIONSHIP OF CHAIRMAN TO BOARD MEMBERS

The CEO of a business corporation is typically chairman of its board. The chairman of the board in a nonprofit organization is not its CEO, and this leads to differences in his relationship with board members (unless the chairman's position is recognized as being primarily ceremonial). The chairman of a nonprofit board selects the chairmen and members of board committees, develops his own ideas for new initiatives, and screens ideas coming from trustees to a greater degree than does the chairman of the board of a business corporation (always obtaining agreement in principle from the CEO, as mentioned above).

The chairman is also the leader of the board, setting its tone; making clear what is expected of the members, both financially and in other ways; and selling them on the organization's virtues. He tries to explain the values that are important in the particular organization. This is much more complicated than in a business organization, in which profitability is a dominant value.

Board members of nonprofit organizations are volunteers, they have diverse interests, and their motivation for participating in the organization's work varies. Although they are presumably mature individuals, their feathers can get ruffled for unintended slights. One of the chairman's unpleasant responsibilities is to deal with disgruntled members.

We believe that the chairman can obtain maximum productivity from the board if he does three things:

1. *Reinforces motivation.* The primary motivation of most board members is to be helpful to an importnat community enterprise. The chairman should remind the board of the ways the organization is carrying out its mission.

2. *Educates.* A participating, useful board member needs to be educated in the special and usually unfamiliar nature of the work that the organization does.

3. *Assigns work.* If a board member has nothing to do, he is likely to lose interest.

DECISION MAKING

Financial Decisions

Although the success of a nonprofit organization is not measured by the amount of its income, the board does have a responsibility for assuring that the budget is balanced, on average and in the long run. If current spending policies lead to an undue debt burden, the board must insist on a change in these policies. If a balanced budget is unlikely with the present relationship be-

tween attainable revenues and necessary expenses, then the
board must insist on appropriate action. This action may include
retrenchment, finding additional fund sources, or, in the extreme, liquidation. Managements naturally want to hang on to
the bitter end, and this can lead to bankruptcy, an unnecessary
waste of assets, and a loss of the community's respect for all concerned, including the members of the board.

The board's responsibility to maintain the financial integrity
of the organization is obvious. It may explain why members of
the board of nonprofit organizations are typically called trustees
rather than directors. The need for fund raising is also obvious,
as is the ceremonial aspect of certain types of boards activities.
In addition to these functions, the board deals with certain other
matters of substance.

CEO Appointment and Evaluation

The board selects the chief excutive officer. There is a well-
known cliche about college and university governance: the function of a governing board is to select the president and then back
him, period. Much harm has resulted when boards took this as
their only function relating to management.[1]

Along with the unquestioned authority to select the CEO goes
the implicit responsibility to ensure that the CEO is performing
satisfactorily—and if not, to require corrective action or termi-
nation. In recent years, formal procedures for evaluating CEOs
have become common, particularly in colleges. If not done properly, the evaluation can be so threatening that it does more harm
than good. If done carefully, however, the CEO can gain useful
insights. He can learn how to perform better and obtain a clearer
understanding of what the board expects.

[1]For a perceptive analysis of the job of a college president, see Michael D. Cohen
and James G. March, *Leadership and Ambiguity*, A general report prepared for
the Carnegie Commission on Higher Education (New York, McGraw Hill, 1974).

Unlike the situation in business organizations, the CEO of a nonprofit organization typically is not expected to develop his or her successor. Thus, when the time comes to select a new CEO, the board usually starts from scratch. Unless there happens to be an obvious candidate, the search can be time consuming.

Program Planning

Neither business nor nonprofit boards should meddle in the day-to-day operations of the organization. A college board should not criticize the content of a particular course or the conduct of a particular faculty member. An orchestra board should not require that particular works be played. As part of its responsibility for the long-run well-being of the organization, however, the board can organize reviews of programs, perhaps with outside assistance. Recommendations resulting from these reviews can, if the parties involved concur, lead to changes in th. general direction of the organization or changes in some important part of it. (If the involved parties do not concur, the CEO has a problem, but it is the CEO's problem, not the board's.)

The board decides on major changes in programs, usually based on the recommendations of the CEO: the addition or discontinuance of an academic department in a college, a school in a university, or a medical service in a hospital; a new concert series in an arts organization; the type of service or target population of a welfare organization. The line between these major decisions, which are the board's responsibility, and matters that the board should avoid is difficult to draw. Generally, the board should lean in the direction of not interfering with ongoing operations, despite the temptation to do otherwise.

An exception to this generalization applies to nonprofit organizations whose management is inexperienced in business. In these organizations, board members can become heavily involvec. in business matters, and their participation will be welcomed, rather than viewed as meddling, if they have the proper attitude.

CONCLUSION

There is a basic similarity between boards of business and non-profit organizations in that they both are responsible for maintaining their organization's viability. However, a nonprofit organization is *not* a business, the CEO of a nonprofit organization is *not* chairman of the board, its board members are volunteers, and the organization's performance cannot be measured by profitability. These differences lead to significant differences in the way nonprofit boards operate. In well run organizations, CEOs, board chairmen, and board members recognize these differences and behave accordingly.

CASE
Bingham College—A Fundamental Disagreement

Martin Hoyt resigned as chairman of the board of Bingham College in 1983 because of a disagreement with the president. Looking back, he wondered whether his actions over the past few years had been correct.

Background.   Bingham College was a hundred-year-old, co-educational, liberal arts college of 2,000 students. In recent years its reputation had improved substantially, and it was generally regarded as being one of the top 100 liberal arts colleges (out of 1,300 colleges). Its endowment per student was one of the 50 largest.

Martin Hoyt received his A.B. from Bingham in 1940. After military service in World War II, he attended Stanford Business School, receiving both an M.B.A. and a doctoral degree. He taught briefly at Stanford and then joined a prestigious management consulting firm. He had consulting engagements with many educational institutions. He left the firm in 1960 to become a vice president of a large manufacturing company with headquarters in New York City. In 1975 he was made executive vice president and chief operating officer of that company.

Hoyt joined the board of Bingham College in 1955 and served continuously thereafter, except for a one-year hiatus in 1967; such a hiatus was required by the bylaws after 12 years of service. At various times he had been chairman of the educational policy committee and of the budget committee. He became chairman of the board in 1978.

Early in 1977, the president of Bingham announced that he planned to retire in June 1978. Hoyt was named chairman of the search committee, which consisted of seven trustees, two faculty members, and two students. The committee compiled a list of 400 names; some had been suggested by trustees and alumni, but most were people who had responded to advertisements. With the help of a retired college president who was hired to check references and obtain other information, the list was narrowed to 20. Members of the search committee visited each of these candidates, and their findings were discussed at length. The list was then narrowed to five. Each of these five, and their spouses, visited the campus for two days, talking with the full search committee and other groups.

Committees of the faculty, administration, alumni, and students had been formed to advise the search committee. Each of these committees enthusiastically endorsed Frank Tompkins for president. The faculty committee went so far as to report that it had no second choice; if Tompkins was not selected, the search should be reopened. The search committee was equally enthusiastic, and by an unanimous decision recommended Tompkins to the full board. He was elected president in February 1978, took office July 1, and was inaugurated in October.

Tompkins was a scientist, age 50, who for the past eight years had been director of a government research organization with 2,000 employees that was one of the National Institutes of Health. With the coming of the Carter administration in 1977, he was given to understand that the President wanted to replace him.

The Problem. By 1977, it was apparent that difficult times lay ahead for colleges. Students who would attend college in the 1980s and 1990s had already been born, and the demographics showed that the college-age population, which had increased rapidly in the 1960s and 1970s, would plateau in 1978, start to decline in 1982, and continue to decline until 1995, at which time the total college-age population would be only 75 percent of the 1978 peak.

In the late 1970s, most colleges and universities were aware of this situation, and some had already begun to react. Some institutions increased their marketing activities. Others introduced programs designed to attract adults from their local communities. Others modified their curriculums in various ways. Still others, although making no specific changes in curriculum, reduced tenure appointments and trimmed overhead, to increase their flexibility to respond to a decline in enrollment.

The Bingham College search committee had asked each of the finalists how he would address the problem of the declining college population. Tompkins said that he was not knowledgeable enough about higher education in general or Bingham in particular to answer the question.

In the fall of 1978, Tompkins arranged a two-day retreat of key trustees, faculty members, administrators, and student leaders. One of the topics discussed briefly was the demographic problem. The consensus seemed to be that Bingham's reputation was such that it could continue to enroll 2,000 students of high caliber.

Hoyt's Analysis. Hoyt did not share this view (although he did not say so at the retreat). He felt that the Ivy League universities and the dozen or so first-tier liberal arts colleges would continue to attract students because of their reputations, and that 90 percent or more of their students would go on to graduate or professional schools. The 1,000 or so colleges that did not have outstanding reputations would seek new ways to compete. Most would survive, but some would fold.

Bingham was not quite in the top tier. About 60 percent of its graduates went on to graduate or professional school, but 40 percent went directly to work. Although applications were currently about eight times the size of an entering class, the number of fully qualified applicants was only about three times the number needed to fill a class. The margin of safety was not as great as the number of applicants indicated because 50 percent of admitted applicants would enroll at another college. Presumably, a similar situation existed at the other 20 or so colleges in the second tier with whom Bingham competed.

As Hoyt saw it, therefore, the first-tier colleges would maintain their enrollment by taking students who otherwise would go to colleges like Bingham. Some additional candidates would become available from colleges that went bankrupt, but the second-tier colleges would be competing vigorously for them. Moreover, tuition at many of these colleges was about two-thirds the tuition at colleges like Bingham, and some students who would be acceptable to Bingham might decide to attend a state university, where the tuition was only about one-third of Bingham's.

Colleges like Bingham would therefore be squeezed from three directions: from the top-tier colleges, from increasing competition from their peers, and from state universities. Whether they could attract a student body comparable in quality to the present student body was doubtful. If the perceived quality declined, the college's reputation would suffer, and this would in turn hurt future applications, perhaps so much as to be catastrophic.

Hoyt thought that Bingham had an advantage that could be exploited. For many years it had offered a major in business administration; this was unusual for a top liberal arts college. In the 1960s and 1970s, the enrollment in this major increased rapidly, becoming second only to English. Since the mission of a liberal arts college was presumably something other than job-related education, the faculty insisted that the major be viewed in this context. Hoyt thought that this emphasis should change and that Bingham should promote the idea that it prepared students for business, and perhaps for other fields as well. He reasoned that the probable decrease in the number of students attending Bingham as preparation for graduate school could be offset by an increase in students who intended to go to work immediately after college.

Discussions, 1978–1982. In 1978 and 1979, Hoyt raised the demographic problem with Tompkins on several occasions, but Tompkins remained noncommittal. In June 1979, Hoyt prepared a memorandum describing the situation in more detail. In it, he stressed the need for fairly quick action because a relatively long time was required to change the public's perception of a college. He showed the memorandum only to Tompkins and to Homer Pottle, vice chairman of the board.

Tompkins continued to be noncommittal, and in 1980 Hoyt stopped discussing the issue. Hoyt did learn that the director of admissions had views similar to his own, but in 1980 that officer died of a heart attack.

In 1981 Hoyt decided that the matter should be brought to a head and so advised Tompkins. Tompkins suggested that Hoyt's 1979 memorandum be discussed with the eight faculty department heads. Such a meeting took place on a Sunday afternoon. Hoyt went through a revised version of his memorandum (it was collected after the meeting), and a four-hour discussion ensued. The general feeling was that any move in the direction of a job-related curriculum was inappropriate. One faculty member went so far as to characterize the proposal as a plan to teach typing and shorthand.

Subsequently, Hoyt discussed the proposal with the joint faculty–trustee educational policy committee. There was some support for it from a minority of trustee members. There was practically no support from the faculty. Tompkins said little at this meeting.

The chairman of the educational policy committee reported on this meeting to the full board of 25 members in January 1982. Neither Hoyt nor Tompkins took part in the ensuing, brief discussion. The board took no action.

It became clear to Hoyt that Tompkins shared the faculty's concern that an emphasis on job-related courses would damage Bingham's reputation as a leading liberal arts college, particularly to students who planned to pursue professional or graduate education. Tompkins had become committed to an alternative strategy, consisting of (1) a greatly expanded marketing effort, approximately doubling the size of the admissions office; and (2) a program to upgrade physical facilities to make the campus more attractive. In order to finance the renovation program, the college issued $10 million of long-term bonds, the first substantial borrowing in its history. Hoyt went along with both policies but was convinced they were inadequate.

The Resignation.   After the January 1982 board meeting, Hoyt decided that his views were incompatible with the president's and that he should resign as chairman. Throughout this period, Hoyt had kept Homer Pottle, the vice chairman, advised of his discussions about the demographic problem. Pottle indicated that he tended to side with the president and that he would be willing to become chairman. After checking with many board members, Hoyt was convinced that this move was agreeable to the board. At the June 1982 board meeting he announced his retirement as of January 1983, giving as his reason the belief that a chairman should serve only a five-year stint. Pottle was elected chairman as of January.

Hoyt continued as a board member. (As a former chairman he was exempt from the 12-year limitation on continuous service.) He was careful not to raise questions about the demographic problem, either publicly or informally.

As of 1984, college enrollments had followed the predicted pattern except that total enrollment in fall 1983 was equal to that of fall 1982, rather than dropping slightly as originally predicted. Bingham's applications and enrollment held steady throughout this period. In his report to the board in October 1983, the president said that $\frac{1}{4}$ of the period from the population peak to its bottom in 1995 had already passed and that the college had survived this period in excellent shape.

Our Comment on Bingham College

Board members with whom we discussed this case were sharply divided.

A few felt strongly that the situation should never have arisen. Hoyt proposed to change the curriculum, they said, and one thing that the trustees must not do is meddle with the curriculum; this is the province of the faculty. At most, Hoyt should have described his plan to the president in 1978 and asked the president to sound out the faculty on it. When the faculty expressed no interest, as the narrative indicated it was almost sure to do, that should have ended the matter.

Another group felt that Hoyt acted properly in raising the issue, that he had done all that he legitimately should have done, and that when he realized that he was not going to convince the president, he should have ceased his campaign, as he did. This group viewed his resignation as strictly a personal matter. If Hoyt felt uncomfortable in his relationship with the president, which was understandable, he should have resigned. If he had been able to put this matter behind him, he should have had no qualms about staying on.

The third view was that Hoyt, experienced in educational issues and a graduate and long-time trustee, had an obligation to push his views much harder than he did. One person said: "He pussyfooted around for three years, and let the lengthy period that would be required to implement a new policy slip by. If his view is correct, Bingham will feel the impact in a year or two, but then it will be too late to do anything about it." The general view of this third group was that the chairman had an obligation to the long-term future of his college that was more important than his obligation to support the new president. He should have lobbied hard for his proposal with board members, in every possible way, and should have participated actively in the crucial board meeting. One person went so far as to say that Hoyt should have told the board that he felt so strongly that he planned to resign if his plan was not adopted.

Those who agreed with Hoyt's action thought that any more overt activity, and especially a threat to resign, would place the president in an untenable position. Because the majority of the faculty tended to support the president's view (or perhaps because the president reflected the faculty's view), bringing the issue out into the open could have serious repercussions.

Suppose Hoyt were successful in obtaining board approval. If the president agreed to implement the plan, the faculty would claim that he was kowtowing to the uninformed lay views of the board, most of whose members did not appreciate the true function of a liberal arts college. If the president continued to oppose a plan that the board favored, friction could develop between the president and the board, and between the faculty and the board. In these circumstances, the president, selected after a thorough search and highly respected, might resign. The lengthy process of presidential search would start again, and by the time the next president had been selected and had become sufficiently familiar with the situation to act, Bingham could be in the midst of the demographic crisis.

Both groups recognized that there was no way of telling whether the president's policies would succeed. The proof would come a few years down the road. If these policies turned out to be inadequate, it might be too late to do anything. Nevertheless, it was not surprising that the majority of the board supported the president; trustees are taught that this was their function, in the absence of convincing evidence that he was wrong.

Our own view is that although Hoyt's analysis may have been

correct, the strong opposition from the president, most faculty leaders, and the majority of the board made his position untenable. Therefore he probably was right to resign as chairman, and he certainly was right to do so in a way that did not lead to a schism. Whether he should continue as a board member depends on his personal views. If he thought he could contribute in other ways, fine. If he harbored resentment about his defeat, the sooner he left, the better.

CASE
Sayre International Center—
Financial Responsibility

In the spring of 1980, the board of directors of Sayre International Center found itself in an awkward situation. The preliminary budget estimate for the year beginning July 1, 1980, indicated that a 14 percent increase in room rates would be required to break even for the year. This increase was unacceptable to Sayre Center residents, who maintained that any increase would impose severe hardship on many of them. Nevertheless, after two years of operating deficits, and with the necessity of making large expenditures for deferred maintenance, some board members believed it was important that Sayre's financial affairs be straightened out. Lewis Goldsmith, a board member and chairman of the finance committee, was the man in the middle.

Background. Sayre Center was an independent organization that offered students a residence center on the campus of a large midwestern state university. The center's building had been built in 1925, financed by a gift from the Sayre family, who had accumulated a substantial fortune in the automobile industry. Rather than build the building and give it to the university, the Sayres (with the university's concurrence) created a nonprofit corporation, and the corporation built Sayre Center on property deeded to it by the university. The building, which cost $2 million and which was a landmark on the campus, included dormitory and dining facilities for 500 students.

Sayre Center was more than a student dormitory. The Sayre family's objective was to provide an environment for foreign students so that they could live and study with American students under conditions that would foster understanding among peoples of different cultures, races, and nations. Accordingly, the building included a large hall for social functions, a well-appointed and comfortable library, a coffee shop, and other rooms and amenities to encourage interaction among foreign and American student residents. In fact, many university-wide international functions were held at Sayre.

According to the terms of the Sayre grant, Sayre Center was an independent, nonprofit corporation, with its own board of directors. The president of the university was ex-officio its chairman. In 1980, there were 16 board members, mostly prominent, active university alumni. They included a number of business and professional men and several women alumnae who were active in university and civic affairs. Three faculty members were on the board.

In accordance with a practice initiated in 1967, the board included two students, who were elected each year by the residents of Sayre Center. In addition to the two student board members, Sayre residents regularly selected student representatives to participate on various board committees concerned with the center's activities and operations. Two students served as representatives to the finance committee. Although these students had no vote, they regularly participated in committee meetings.

Over the years, Sayre had become an integral part of the university's social and educational structure. About half of the 500 residents were foreign students, and the others were Americans. Sayre maintained a small, full-time staff, which worked with the foreign residents on their orientation, and which developed social and cultural programs to encourage interaction between

American and foreign students. These programs were generally quite successful, and student life at Sayre Center was considered to be an enriching experience.

By the mid-1970s, the Sayre Center building was 50 years old. In recent years the maintenance program had been inadequate, and in 1980 the building needed considerable rehabilitation. It was conservatively estimated that expenditures of $300,000 per year would be required to rehabilitate and then to adequately maintain the building and its facilities and furnishings. This was almost twice the average annual maintenance expenditures for the past five years.

At the same time, inflation was creating problems for students, especially those from developing countries. There were, in fact, a number of unfortunate instances of fine foreign students having to leave Sayre and either return home or move to substandard accommodations because of their inability to meet Sayre's room and board charges. This became an emotional issue with Sayre residents. In fact, the night before the April 1980 finance committee meeting, Sayre residents held a meeting at which there was a strong expression that room rates not be increased and that board rates be increased only to reflect increased food costs. A petition was signed by 206 students, and the student representatives to the finance committee were instructed to present it to the committee and to lobby vigorously against any larger increase.

The April 1980 Meeting. Immediately after chairman Goldsmith called the April 1980 finance committee meeting to order, the student representatives asked for the floor. The request was granted. The spokesman made his presentation in a calm, deliberate fashion. He presented the petition and stated the student position that raising room rates would create hardships for those whom Sayre Center was intended to serve. He said that Sayre was in danger of becoming an "elitist house," affordable only by wealthy students.

Goldsmith thanked the students, said that he and other board members respected their views, but pointed out that it was the board's obligation to make sure that Sayre was financially viable over the long term, so that it could carry on its mission with future generations of students.

Thereafter, the committee turned its attention to examining each category of revenue and expense, comparing the budget projections with current and past performance. Goldsmith was impressed with the students' knowledge and understanding of the numbers.

While there were some minor gives and takes in the budget, in the end it came down to rate increases versus inadequate expenditures for maintenance and rehabilitation of the building. It was concluded that a rate increase of 6 percent would be required for the dining room just to cover projected increases in food costs.

While there was no well-defined market rate for dormitory rooms in the community, Sayre Center was clearly neither at the top nor the bottom of the prevailing rates. Over the previous three years rates had been increased, but not to the same degree as other dormitories, so far as could be determined. The university operated some dormitories, and their increases over the preceding year, compared with Sayre, were as follows:

	1977	1978	1979	1980
Sayre	6%	7%	7%	9%
University	8%	10%	11%	12%

Information was not available concerning the university's plans for 1981. For several years Sayre's rooms had been filled, and there was a waiting list.

The students pointed out that the single largest budget increase was for building maintenance and rehabilitation, projected for $300,000 in 1981. If room rates were maintained at the 1980 level and the $300,000 was spent on the building, the budget would show an operating deficit of $175,000. To bring this deficit to zero would require a room rate increase of 14 percent. The students regarded this increase as unacceptable.

One student suggested that there should be a fund-raising program to help finance the rehabilitation of Sayre Center. Goldsmith said that over the years there had been a modest fundraising program but that it had been only marginally successful. Individuals had made gifts to refurbish the library and several of the common rooms, and a foundation had given money to remodel the main entrance. Thus far, however, Sayre had been unable to generate a program of regular contributions. Moreover, he said, he doubted that contributions would ever be a dependable source and certainly could not be counted on in the immediate future.

The finance committee needed to make a recommendation to the Sayre board at its May meeting. Also, room and board rates for the coming year needed to be published within a few weeks.

At the end of the formal meeting, Goldsmith dismissed the student representatives, thanking them for their contributions, and the four board members met with the director of Sayre Center, Conrad Gullixson. Gullixson had been Sayre's director for 18 years and was a respected member of the university community. He was obviously concerned and upset. He was fearful of the student reaction if the board voted an increase anywhere near 14 percent. The two student members of the board of directors would, he believed, feel obliged to oppose a significant increase, and this would create an unfortunate rift between the board and the student residents.

One of the directors, on the other hand, said he thought the time had come to take some rather drastic action. Sayre couldn't continue to operate at a deficit and at the same time permit the physical plant to deteriorate. He thought some lost ground should be made up and that an increase of at least 15 percent should be put into effect. The other two board members thought the increase should be made more gradually, but agreed that a significant increase was in order.

Goldsmith felt that the committee was looking to him for a recommendation.

Our Comment on Sayre International Center

Constituents of nonprofit organizations have a tendency to avoid facing economic realities. The board must be hard headed in countering these tendencies. In this situation, there appears to be no viable alternative to raising room rates. Other possibilities seem unrealistic. There is always a temptation to attempt a special fund-raising effort, but this had been tried without success. If the renovation was a one-shot proposition, it might have been financed with borrowing, with a repayment schedule that would spread the pain over a number of future years. However, Goldsmith foresaw the need for large renovation expenditures for several more years, and borrowing would simply be a way of postponing the eventual repayment. We therefore think that Goldsmith should insist on a substantial rate increase.

In doing so, Goldsmith runs the risk of a strong student reaction, including violence. We think that this risk is worth taking. Students living in Sayre might protest, but their rents are already lower than those in some other university dormitories, and they are unlikely to gain university-wide support. If some students carry the protest to the point of moving out, there are evidently others waiting to take their place. Since Sayre rates have been increasing at a slower rate than those in university dormitories, it is likely that even a 14 percent increase will not cause them to be out of line. The increase does favor the well-to-do students, but there seems to be nothing that can be done about that. As a minor tactic, Goldsmith might shift some of the increase to the board charges, thus making the increase in room rates less than 14 percent.

Goldsmith, and other board members, must expect to invest a

considerable amount of time explaining the need for the increased rate to disgruntled groups. Unfortunately, there seems to be no alternative.

The case points up the advantages of student participation in governance under the right circumstances. Students were given an opportunity to make their case, they did so in a mature manner, and this should make the board's decision more palatable.

The case also suggests two basic policies that often are not given adequate consideration in nonprofit organizations.

First, it is dangerous to accept funds for a building in which a peripheral activity will be conducted without also obtaining endowment that will finance the operating expenses of that activity. Some universities require a dollar of additional endowment for each dollar spent on bricks and mortar in such buildings.

Second, each year's revenues should ordinarily be sufficient to finance that year's expenses. There is a natural temptation to put off the day of reckoning, to push the problem forward so that it becomes the concern of some future board. In the Sayre situation, this would have been unfair to future boards and to future students as well. Future students would inevitably have to pay additional fees to make up for the past deficits.

10

Trends

In this final chapter we suggest what seem to us to be likely developments affecting directors and their responsibilities. Any such attempt to predict the future starts with an analysis of the present, and the forecaster must try to distinguish between two quite different types of movements. Some movements are trends, and their future direction will be continuation of the present curve. Other movements are cycles, and in the future they will swing in an opposite direction from their behavior at present. Moreover, some trends will emerge on the basis of factors not currently understood.

BOARD STANDARDS OF CONDUCT

Boards of directors will be held to increasingly high standards of conduct.

Although public attention goes in cycles, with headline-hunting congressional investigations followed by periods of relative indifference, expectations tend to be higher with each cycle, and the current expectations are vastly higher than those in the early 20th century. This upward trend is likely to continue. In response to society's expectations, the board will pay closer

attention to the ethical, legal, and social standards of the corporation. It will require that these standards be articulated and will
see to it that procedures are in place (and are effective) for providing reasonable assurance that the standards are complied
with.

The audit committee probably will continue to have the primary responsibility for monitoring compliance, but other committees and the full board will signal the importance of these
standards by both words and deeds.

THE BOARD'S OBJECTIVES

*Directors will increasingly recognize that they are responsible for
the long-run best interests of the corporation, not merely the interests of the shareowners. The courts, legislative bodies, the SEC,
and the public gradually will accept the same view.*

Many textbooks on management and finance state that the
board's responsibility is to represent the shareowners, to maxi-
mize the shareowners' wealth, or some similar phrase that fo-
cuses solely on the shareowners' interest. There is an assumption
that shareowners are individuals who invest in a company in
order to become part owners and that they elect directors to protect their ownership interest, which is a long-run interest. Case
law tends to accept the same assumption.

At one time this assumption may have been reasonably valid.
Today, however, pension funds, endowment funds, mutual funds,
and similar pools of money hold a high percentage of equity investments in public companies. Managers of these funds have
no loyalty to, nor personal interest in, the corporation. They will
sell anytime they judge that their money will earn more if in-
vested in another security. In a public corporation today, shareowner equity is merely one source of capital. Most shareowners
are not interested in owning a piece of the corporation; they are
interested primarily in near-term financial gain.

In these circumstances, the board's responsibility to the shareowner is not much different from its responsibility to banks and other lenders. Both shareowners and lenders are providers of funds. The board is fundamentally responsible for the health of the corporation. Increasingly, boards will think as much about the interests of employees as they do about the interests of funds providers, and they also will think about the corporation as a responsible member of society.

In many instances, boards legitimately resist unfriendly take-over attempts because they judge that the acquiring group of "financial entrepreneurs" might alter the company in ways that are not in the best long-term interests of the corporation and of its various constituencies. For example, they might simply sell off assets, pocket the money, and leave the company in ruins. Whose long-term interests are being served?

LITIGATION

There will be fewer successful law suits against boards.

The current status of public liability law is rapidly becoming intolerable. Judgments against defendants in liability suits have become so excessive and the costs to society so high as to force the legal system in the future to provide more rational decisions. Some legislative bodies are already aware of this situation and have begun to pass laws to correct it; many more will do so.

This tendency will moderate the level of concern that directors now have with respect to their personal liability.

STRATEGY FORMULATION

The board will increasingly assure itself that the management has a well-defined and well-thought-out set of strategies.

The task of the corporation will become increasingly complex. Competition is likely to intensify. To remain competitive, companies will become increasingly global in their outlook. Companies are divesting business units that don't "fit"; they are trimming fat; they are producing abroad and sourcing from abroad; they are making major investments in manufacturing facilities. Decisions on these matters involve major issues of corporate strategy, and as such they should be dealt with at the board level. This requires that the board be assured that the company has a sound and up-to-date strategy and that management's decisions are consistent with this strategy.

Most boards deal with corporate strategy on a full-board basis. A few have strategy committees that probe this area more deeply than can be done with the full board. As companies restructure or refocus their activities in response to more intense global competition, more companies will probably create separate strategy committees.

DIRECTORS' ACTIVITIES

Directors will discharge their increased responsibility without a corresponding increase in the time they spend.

As the function of the typical board continues to shift from a largely ceremonial one to active participation in decision making and in oversight of corporate standards, the information needed by directors will change accordingly. At present, neither directors nor management understand clearly just what the new information needs are, however. In order to be on the safe side, management currently tends to furnish more information than is needed, both prior to the board meeting and as a part of the board meeting. Through trial and error, optimum information needs will gradually be agreed to, and the power of computers and advanced communication facilities will provide directors with better and more timely information than has been the case in the past. This will save time and permit directors to devote more attention to the policy issues that they increasingly will face.

SELECTION OF BOARD MEMBERS

Companies will have to work harder to maintain good boards.

Time commitments and the added responsibilities of board membership will make it increasingly difficult to attract and keep qualified outside board members. Potential directors will become more selective in making board commitments. As a consequence, board chairmen and nominating committees will devote more attention to seeking out good board members. Moreover, individuals will tend to be attracted to, and to remain on, boards which stimulate them and on which they feel their contribution is useful.

Compensation, while not a major factor in attracting good board members, will increase. It will increasingly become a measure of the significance attached to board membership.

COMPOSITION OF THE BOARD

Boards will be more assertive in influencing board membership.

Boards will continue to be essentially self perpetuating. The trend toward increased involvement by the board in the selection of new board members will accelerate, with more boards using active nominating committees. Board membership will become increasingly diverse and will include more women and minorities as the pool of qualified candidates increases.

Ratification of board membership by shareowners will continue to be a pro forma act (except in highly unusual circumstances). We regard as unworkable the proposal to have some board members selected by unions, as is done in certain European countries. We think it even more undesirable to have a representative of government on the board. Self-perpetuating boards are the norm in both business and nonprofit organizations. We think this practice is superior to any alternative.

RELATION TO THE CEO

Directors will become more independent of the CEO.
In recent years, through the activities of audit and nominating committees, outside directors have tended increasingly to act independently of the CEO. We believe this trend will continue, and that directors, irrespective of board committees, will become more sensitive to their responsibility of being objective and independent of the CEO.

Independence, however, does not imply conflict. There will continue to be a commonality of purpose between the board and the CEO, and the board will continue to refrain from meddling in operating matters.

NONPROFIT ORGANIZATIONS

Members of boards of trustees will play a more important role in nonprofit organizations. Health care organizations have serious financial problems as their basis for pricing shifts from cost reimbursement to a fair value for services rendered. Colleges and universities have the problem of a declining student population. Arts organizations can count less on the support of wealthy patrons. Consequently, these and other types of nonprofit organizations must become more businesslike in order to survive. Their boards will emphasize the importance of sound business methods. Trustees will nevertheless continue to serve as volunteers, without compensation.

Another consequence of the financial strains will be that the influence of professionals (e.g., physicians, artists, professors, engineers) will decrease to the extent that their views conflict with the requirements of financial viability. (For example, university faculties will not be able to offer as many courses whose enrollment does not pay their own way; arts organizations will not plan activities beyond those that can be financed with current resources.)

CONCLUSION

If these changes come to pass, as we think they will, the work of the director will be more challenging, more important to society, and therefore even more interesting than typically is the case now. Since we are approaching retirement, we cannot expect to participate in these developments for many more years. We wish all the best to those who will carry on.

Appendix
Corporate Directors in Japan[1]

The process of corporate governance, as well as the composition and the role of the board of directors, in Japanese business is very different from that of U.S. corporations. Boards in Japan are composed almost exclusively of insiders elected by shareowners at a formal and legal shareowners meeting, as the Japanese Companies Act requires.

If governance is considered to be the process by which owners of the corporation exercise influence over its management, however, the Japanese board can hardly be considered to perform this role. Ownership, as distinct from management, is not represented on boards. The corporate governance process appears to take place behind the scenes between the senior corporate official and the major institutional shareowners.

To understand the role of the board of directors and the governance process in Japan, the reader should be aware of two significant differences between major U.S. and Japanese businesses.

First, by contrast with large, publicly owned U.S. corporations, the ownership of major Japanese companies is concentrated in the hands of a few large institutions. A typical example is a large chemical company in which individuals comprise more

[1]Reprinted from Charles A. Anderson, "Corporate Directors in Japan," *Harvard Business Review*, May-June 1984.

than 98 percent of the shareowners but own less than 17 percent of the shares. Financial institutions—mainly banks and insurance companies—own 59 percent of the shares. Ten of these institutions own nearly 44 percent of the equity. Moreover, banks with large equity interests are also the major lenders to the corporation.

This pattern of concentration of both equity and debt in the hands of a few banks and financial institutions is common in Japanese industry. Although there are today a growing number of individuals who own shares in Japanese corporations, they still do not constitute a significant ownership element. As one Japanese chairman told me, "Japan does not have individual capitalists like you have in the United States."

Second, as is well known, there exists in Japan a degree of unity between management and labor not found in U.S. business. There is a sense that a Japanese corporation—its employees and managers—is a social entity of its own.

As a consequence, there is little confrontation between the workers and management, and all of the board members regard themselves as being just as responsible for the interests of the employees as for the interests of the shareowners. Many senior Japanese managers have come up through the ranks and have been union leaders at one time or another. Thus, they seem to feel at least as obligated to the workers as to the owners of the corporation. This notion is widely accepted.

One Japanese chairman remarked, "We don't want an outsider on our board. We don't need a watch-dog." This sentiment appears to stem from the widely held concept that the corporation is a social unit in which everyone has a role and a stake. An outsider who is not a part of that social entity simply does not belong, whether he (read "he or she") represents owners or not.

In December 1983, I made a trip to Japan during which I talked with senior executives in a leading trading company and five large companies in the computer, steel, and chemical industries. Also, I interviewed a dozen or more professional people who are knowledgeable about Japanese boards and how they function.

With the foregoing as background, augmented by my interest

in and experience with U.S. boards, I shall undertake to describe in this article some of the most interesting aspects of corporate governance and the board of directors in Japan.

COMPOSITION OF BOARDS

Under the Japanese Companies Act, a corporation is required to have a board made up of at least three directors. The board has the power to make decisions on matters concerning the operation of the business, but the board itself does not execute such decisions.

In practice, Japanese boards consist almost entirely of corporate senior managers; in major corporations, the number of board members ranges from 20 to 50. By contrast with U.S. boards, in which each board member has equal status, Japanese boards have a considerable hierarchy of directors. Positions represented on the board might be chairman, president, executive vice president, senior managing director, managing director, and director.

A group of the senior directors designated by the full board as "representative directors" have the legal power to represent the company as a whole and to act for and on behalf of the company with third parties. Boards may have from two or three members to as many as half their membership as representative directors.

One Japanese company, for example, has 49 directors drawn from all of the company's operating and staff divisions. Nearly half (an unusually high percentage) are representative directors. The full board meets monthly, while the representative directors meet weekly. The representative directors, most of whom are located at the company's Tokyo headquarters, are, in fact, the company's senior officers. They consider and make decisions regarding major policy and operating matters, which they then recommend to the full board. Since the full board consists of corporate officers junior to the representative directors, it rarely, if ever, fails to approve such recommendations.

A good deal has been written about participation and consensus in Japanese business. In the foregoing example, it appears that both the representative directors and the full board are part of the participatory process whereby management reaches a consensus. In fact, one official of this company referred to the famous *ringi* system in which each director actually "signs off" on major corporate decisions. Presumably, such signing off takes place only after thorough discussion. Thereafter, each director is expected to give loyal and wholehearted support to the decision.

It seems, then, that full board consideration of an issue is an important device for fostering communication within the management group. Moreover, action by the board is a formal act of concurrence and commitment by senior management.

While Japanese law mandates that each corporation must have a board and each board must elect one or more representative directors, the law does not otherwise provide for selection of corporate officers. However, positions such as chairman, president, executive vice president, and so on are given by vote of the full board to certain of the representative directors. The title "president" is generally given to the representative director who is regarded as the most important person in the company. The "chairman" is most often the senior representative director— probably the former president who is now semiretired. Japanese business does not use the term "chief executive officer." It is clear, however, that in most instances the president is the equivalent to the U.S. CEO.

SELECTION OF SUCCESSORS

The process of selecting a new president is, of course, a matter of major moment. On this subject, a well informed Japanese senior corporate officer gave me the following statement:

The actual process of selecting the representative director with the title of president in the first-class enterprises in Japan is for the then retiring president to nominate his successor after consultation with former and retired representative directors with the title of president of the company.

*In certain circumstances, the opinion of the main banks of the company
as to the appointment of the president may be sought.*

*The formalities for selecting the representative director with the title
of president are usually taken at a meeting of the board of directors of
the company held after the general meeting of the shareholders where
the directors of the company shall have been elected.*

It is interesting to note that the legal formalities of selecting
the president are quite similar to the legal process of CEO selection in the United States. In actuality, however, it is clear that
the Japanese board of directors has little, if any, influence over
the decision. Since the board consists entirely of company managers, as noted earlier, it is understandable that their participation is very limited.

The outgoing president plays the dominant role in selecting
his successor. This is, of course, common practice in the United
States. Note, however, an important difference. Because U.S.
boards consist largely of outside directors, a forum exists for review and discussion of this important issue. Moreover, the U.S.
directors, as representatives of the shareowners, have—or at least
can have—an influence in the succession decision. In Japan, with
no representative from the shareowners on the board, no such
forum exists—at least not in a formal or legal sense.

It would be incorrect, however, to conclude that Japanese
ownership has no influence in the selection process. Note the
following sentence from the statement cited earlier regarding selection of the president: "In certain circumstances, the opinion
of the main banks of the company as to the appointment of the
president may be sought."

That is a significant point. While there is no legal obligation
on the part of a retiring president to do so, subtly and informally
he makes certain that the presidential candidate is satisfactory
to at least the largest ownership interests. In my discussions with
corporate presidents, without exception each said that he had
sole responsibility for selecting his successor. In further discussion, however, they also said that they were careful to select
someone who would be supported by the key owners.

In fact, one gets the impression that the succession process in first-line Japanese corporations is really an undertaking among the president, the chairman, and a few important individuals from the leading banks or institutions that have major financial interests in the company. The insider board can never be a forum for dealing with this issue.

Over time the Japanese corporate community has consistently been able to produce and select able leaders for its enterprises. Such success doesn't just happen but stems, as we have seen, from the subtle yet effective, behind-the-scenes interaction between top corporate officials and the persons representing ownership and financial interests.

The process of selecting new directors follows much the same pattern as that of a new president. In this instance, the president, in consultation with a few senior representative directors, selects the potential candidates from among the corporate managers. Again, the president will ensure that the new directors are acceptable to the ownership interests. The slate is then submitted to the shareowners for vote. If the company's shares are traded on the Tokyo Stock Exchange, management is required to submit biographical data on each director in advance of the shareowners meeting.

The presidents and chairmen I interviewed agreed that there are three requisite qualifications for becoming a new director in Japan:

1. That the candidate be recognized as a successful manager of an important department or division of the company and possess demonstrated qualities of leadership.

2. That the candidate have the support of labor. Without exception, each president and chairman made it clear that since one of the roles of the board is to represent employee interests, the directors have to be not only sensitive to the needs of the employees but also acceptable to and supported by them.

3. That the candidate have support of ownership interests.

In my discussions, the Japanese executives placed more emphasis on requisites number one and two than on three. This is not to suggest, however, that approval of the banks or other institutions is less meaningful. More likely, it is just the least visible part of the process.

EVALUATION OF MANAGEMENT

Perhaps the most rigorous test of an effective board in the United States is whether it can make a change in leadership when corporate results are unsatisfactory. Since this requires making a critical appraisal of the president's performance, it is unrealistic to expect that an entirely inside board can accomplish this task. How, then, is this done in Japanese corporations?

The answer again rests in the behind-the-scenes interaction between financial interests and senior management. If it becomes evident to the banks and other institutions having an important stake in the company that a change in management is necessary, a quiet meeting—or meetings—will be held with the less than satisfactory president and he will simply not stand for reappointment. He will gracefully retire and a new president will emerge. The former president may or may not continue as a director. That is the Japanese way—no publicity. But it works.

There is a question as to how the ownership representatives obtain the kind of information they need to make a critical evaluation of a corporate president. Sometimes, of course, the evidence is painfully apparent from public information. In most instances, however, it is not, and the published data need to be supplemented by what would otherwise be considered insider information. This would include, by way of example, detailed financial performance data, market share information, product performance, new product plans, a "feel" as to the extent to which the president has the confidence of the organization, and so on.

How, then, do shareowners, who are not members of the board, obtain this type of insider information? I received one very straightforward response to this question.

The president of one of Japan's largest corporations reported that he quite regularly met informally with the two or three institutions holding major financial stakes in his company. He kept them up to date on the company's progress, informed them of problems, and offered to provide any information they might wish concerning the company's status. This information, which he gave out only on a very selective basis, wasn't made available to individual shareowners. This type of selective disclosure is, of course, not permitted by SEC rules in the United States.

COMPENSATION OF OFFICERS

In addition to selecting CEOs and monitoring their performance, U.S. boards are responsible for making their compensation arrangements. This function includes setting compensation for all corporate officers as well as approving and overseeing bonus plans, stock option plans, and other incentive arrangements. Typically, this responsibility is delegated to the board's compensation committee, which consists of outside directors and which makes its recommendations to the full board.

The U.S. procedure obviously is not applicable to the Japanese board composed of management personnel. How, then, is compensation set for senior management in Japanese corporations?

Legally, the shareowners approve the total amount paid to the full board of directors. This is a lump sum, distribution of which is determined by the board itself. Both practically and legally, this means that Japanese presidents set their own compensation and also determine that of the other directors. It is significant that there is no disclosure as to the amount of payment (either salary or bonus) made to individual directors, including the president. The only amount disclosed is the lump sum paid to the directors as a group.

Traditionally, payments to the directors are kept in line with payments to employees. The president waits to see what pay increase or bonus is approved for employees and then recommends an increase of similar proportion in compensation to the directors. So in practice, compensation to Japanese directors is constrained by what employees receive.

In contrast, the Greyhound Corporation settled a strike with its union employees in late 1983 with a 7.8 percent reduction in wages; at the same time, it was reported that managerial salaries were expected to increase by 7 percent or 8 percent. It seems unlikely that an arrangement of this sort would be acceptable in Japan.

The perception of some Japanese senior executives is that their compensation is low in relation to U.S. standards. While there is no disclosure of individual remuneration in Japan, these executives can easily compare their salaries with those published in the proxy statements of U.S. companies.

One executive predicted that this gap might be troublesome in the future. His company is becoming involved in joint ventures in the United States, and difficulties regarding compensation have sprung up among Japanese executives assigned to these operations. Keeping their compensation in line with their U.S. counterparts puts them far beyond the traditional Japanese scale. Thus, as Japanese companies increasingly work with U.S. companies, this disparity will put pressure on the traditional methods of allotting compensation.

EXAMINATION OF AUDITS

A significant function of a U.S. corporate board is the directors' critical review of financial results and the annual report to shareowners. This is a prime function of the board's audit committee, and for a U.S. company with securities listed on the New York Stock Exchange, all members of the committee are required to be outsiders.

Since Japanese companies (with rare exception) do not have outside board members, it is interesting to note how this function is handled. All major corporations follow the general U.S. practice of having outside professional firms (with similar professional standards as in the United States) audit their accounts and issue statements that certify the acceptability (or otherwise) of their financial statements.

The difference between U.S. and Japanese practice is that the Japanese corporation has no audit committee. Instead, the company relies on "statutory auditors" to monitor both internal corporate accounting and to provide the interface with the outside auditors. The statutory auditors (there may be more than one) are elected by the shareowners in exactly the same process as that used for directors.

Although not directors, they generally attend board meetings and are presumed to have full access to the company's records and reports. They sign off on the company's financial reports to the shareowners, and any disagreement they might have with the internal accounting reports would normally be reported to the company's president.

Corporate management in Japan accepts and respects the independent role of the statutory auditors, who are usually drawn, however, from the corporation's own accounting organization and selected by the corporate leaders. Thus, on the surface at least, this makes them less independent than the typical audit committee of a U.S. board. They are more like an internal auditor in a U.S. corporation.

PARTICIPATION IN POLICYMAKING

U.S. directors are generally regarded as having responsibility for "broad corporate policies." While the degree of involvement varies widely in the United States, most boards at least review and have the right to reject the company's annual plans and budgets. In some instances, they participate actively with management in discussing strategic issues, such as major acquisitions or divestitures, plant expansions, financing plans, and the like. In most cases, management takes the lead and goes to the board only for review and approval.

Some people argue that in such instances the board simply acts as a rubber stamp. Nevertheless, many others regard the review process as a useful and constructive discipline for both management and the outside directors.

The Japanese board, consisting entirely of managers, does not have (at least structurally) a similar process. Management develops plans and policies, and then approves them. There is no linkage to, or participation by, those having ownership interests in the corporation. This inability of ownership to have a voice in decisions affecting their interests must be regarded as a shortcoming of the typical Japanese board.

In practice, however, the president of a Japanese company will obtain the informal concurrence of ownership or financial interests before making a major change in policy. This is especially true in cases in which the implications are great, such as when new capital investment or other financing is required.

The process, the same as that described earlier in the selection of successors discussion, is the informal, behind-the-scenes Japanese way. It seems to work—at least for now. But it depends on actions outside the board function and structure. This weakness of the Japanese system is again traceable to the insider composition of the board.

ACCOMMODATION TO CHANGE

In a little more than one generation following World War II, wartorn Japan built one of the world's most powerful industrial societies—a feat beyond almost everyone's expectations. Obviously, the top corporate leadership structure and governance practices have served the Japanese business community well.

The question now is whether this structure will work as well in the future. Several perceptive Japanese business leaders have reservations in this regard. They discussed with me several trends that they think could either force change or make it desirable.

First, Japanese individuals are increasingly becoming share-owners in Japanese industry. As this trend continues, it is possible that these shareowners will exert pressure to have outsiders on boards to represent the shareowners' interests. Even now, there are nominal interest shareowners making demands and even being disruptive at shareowners meetings. In fact, there is a movement under way intended to restrict such activities by requiring a shareowner to have more than a few shares in the company to qualify for active involvement at meetings.

Second, there is a segment of the Japanese press increasingly engaged in investigative reporting directed at major corporations. The Mitsukoshi Department Store, for example, was a target of the press, which was to some degree responsible for shaping public opinion and bringing pressure on the company directors to remove the president whose personal and ethical conduct became unacceptable to a significant portion of the Japanese community. As scandals of considerable proportion were reported in the press, there was pressure to "do something."

In this instance, there was an outsider on the board who convinced the employee directors to join him in voting for the president's ouster. The story has it that the vote was 20 to 1.

Because of the widespread publicity attendant to this entire episode, one Japanese businessman described it as the noisy, raucous American way of dealing with the problem, not the quiet Japanese way.

Presumably, more outside directors representing the share-owners' interests (both large and small) as well as the public interest would constitute a highly effective response to pressure for change in the future.

Third, while over the past 30 years Japanese business has been dominated by its large industrial complexes, now emerging are small innovative companies, together with the availability of venture capital to nurture them. As these organizations mature, many have the objective of going public. It is unlikely that the boards of these companies will follow the traditional pattern and practices of the Mitsubishis, Mitsuis, and Sumitomos. Instead, the venture capitalists will likely ask for participation at the board level.

Fourth, there is the growing internationalization of Japanese industry, which is taking place in two ways: (1) investors from the world at large are increasingly diversifying their portfolios to include Japanese businesses, and (2) as mentioned earlier, Japanese companies are becoming affiliated in a variety of ways with companies in the United States and Europe. Examples are Toyota's venture with General Motors and Fujitsu's partnership with Amdahl in the computer field. Joint arrangements such as these will almost certainly result not only in a better understanding of different systems but also greater commonality of practice.

Looking to the future (perhaps 10 to 15 years away), I would not be surprised to see Japanese business sprouting new venture companies, engaging in mergers and corporate takeovers, and participating in other corporate practices that characterize corporate communities in other countries. If this happens, I expect that the current, traditional structure of the Japanese board of directors will change, reflecting a need to be responsive to broader and different shareowner interests.

The business leadership in Japan has amply proven its ability to adapt to changing circumstances. There is little doubt in my mind that management will apply the same flexibility to the structure and function of its board of directors.

Index

Acme Energy Company case, 56–59
Acquired companies, boards of, 34
Agee, Bill, 97
Allied Corporation, 97
Analysts, relation with, 177–178
Andrews, Kenneth, 25
Annual meeting, 32
Arbuckle, Ernest C., 95
Atlantic Corporation case, 125–134
AT&T, 173
Audit committee:
  board organization, 6
  functions, 139–153
  internal audit reports, 147–148
  relations with house counsel, 150
  relations with internal audit staff,
    146
  relations with outside auditors,
    145–146
  responsibilities of, 141–142
  staff assistance, 150–151
Auditors:
  non-audit work, 152
  selection of, 151–152
Audits, Japanese corporations, 238

Baldwin-United, 74
Bank of Boston, 74

BarChris case, 139–140
Bendix Corporation, 97
Big bath, 145
Bingham College case, 206–212
Bishop, Joseph, W., Jr., 140
Board activities, 4–6
Board committees, 5–6
Board composition:
  age, 91
  bankers, 90–91
  CEOs, 92
  gender and race, 91
  honorary directors, 109
  Japanese corporations, 131–132
  major shareowners, 92
  nonprofit corporations, 225
  size, 5
  see also Nominating committee
Board information, 50
Board interlocking membership, 105
Board leadership without CEO, 65, 76
Board meetings:
  agenda, 29
  first meeting, 29
  informal activities, 31–32
  impression from minutes, 17–18
  number of, 5, 28
  preparation for, 19, 28–29, 52

Board membership:
  deciding on, 95
  qualifications, 89
  selection of, 61, 93, 99, 225, 234
Board organization, 6
Board responsibilities, 3
Board retirement policy, 97–98, 108
Board review, 52
Board size, 5, 87
Boise Cascade Corporation, 171
Bribery, 149
Business judgment rule, 141
Business Roundtable, 21

Cabot, Louis B., 22
Capco Company case, 74–77
Carborundum Company, 23
Carlson, Robert, 64
Caterpillar Corporation, 171
Certified public accountants, 141–142
Chief executive officer:
  accountability, 3, 48–49
  appraisal of, 21–22
  board attitude toward, 30
  board evaluation of, 64–68
  compensation, see Compensation
  nonprofit organizations, 194–195,
    200–205, 226
  replacement of, 3, 64–68
  role of, 47–56
  succession, see Succession for CEO
  suggestions for, 50–56
  who is not chairman, 54
Clean audit opinion, 142
Cleary Company case, 7–15
Cohen, Michael D., 204 n
Colleges:
  demographic problem, 208
  presidential search, 207–208
Committees, see specific names of
    committees
Commodore International, 71
Compensation:
  board of directors, 123–124
  board responsibilities, 4
  CEO, 111–119
  differing views, 132–133
  guidelines, 112
  incentives, 115–117

Japanese corporations, 236
  policy, 117–119
  use of formulas, 116–117
Compensation committee:
  annual review process, 119–121
  board organization, 5–6
  role of, 111–125, 133–134
Conoco, 34
Continental Illinois Bank, 74
Crises:
  dealing with, 63–74
  preparation for, 20–21

Daniell, Robert, 64
Dayton, Kenneth N., 54 n
Dayton-Hudson, 55
Debt policy, 174–175
Decision-making in nonprofit
    organizations, 203–205
Deere and Company, 88
Directors' duties, 17–35, 222–223
Directors and officers insurance, 140–141
Directors' liabilities, 69
Dividend policy, 171–173, 182–183
Dow Chemical Company, 88
Drohan, Thomas, 55
Drucker, Peter, 1
Du Pont, 34
Duties of board in nonprofit
    organizations, 196

Economic standards, see Standards
Ethical standards, see Standards
Executive committee, 6

Finance committee, 6, 169–180
Financial decision, in nonprofit
    organization, 203–204
Financial information furnished to
    directors, 19–20
Financial policies, review of, 173–174
Financial statements, audit committee
    responsibility for, 142–143
Foreign Corrupt Practices Act, 149
Frank Cavier case, 40–46

Geneen, Harold, 1, 48–49
Goldberg, Arthur, 150
Golden parachutes, 72–73

Governance:
 board function, 1–7
 CEO attitude toward, 47–49
 Japanese corporations, 229–230
 Grady Company case, 180–185
Gray, Harry, 48, 64

Hammer, Armand, 48
Harlan, Neil, 55, 202
Hatfield, Robert, 92
Heinz, H. J., 143
Hewlett, William, 55
Hewlett-Packard Company, 55,
 172–173
Hoover Corporation case, 161–166
Hospital boards, 199
Human resources committee, 124–125

Icahn, Carl, 70
Internal audit, 146–149
International Harvester, 116
Inventory policy, 184–185
Investor relations, 177–178

Japanese boards, 229–241
Jefferson, Edward, 34

Kerr, Clark, 195
Killearn Properties, Inc., 141

Leveraged buyout, 69
Liability insurance, 140–141
LIFO, 184–185
Litigation, 223
Little, Arthur D. Inc., 194
Lockheed Corporation, 74

Mace, Myles, 2, 77, 77 n, 93
Management letter, 147
March, James G., 204 n
Martin Marietta Corporation, 97, 146
Massey-Ferguson, 116
McCardell, Archie, 116
McKesson Corporation, 55
Meddling, 14
Meetings, *see* Board meetings
Menlo Corporation case, 59–62
Miller, Arjay, 112, 150
Minority board members, 199

Nominating committee:
 practices, 93–94, 103–105
 role of, 87–99
Nonprofit organizations:
 authority of CEO, 194–195
 board members, 195–196
 clients and employee members,
  196–197
 composition of board, 197–200
 differences among boards, 194–197
 difficulty of measuring performance,
  197
 minority board members, 197
 relation of board to CEO, 200–203
 relationship of chairman to board
  members, 202–203
 role of board, 193–206, 226

Operations, review of, 21–22

Packard, David, 55
Penn Central Corporation, 21
Pension funds, 178–180, 186–190
Pensions, for directors, 136
Private companies, boards of, 32–34
Program planning, in nonprofit
 organizations, 205–206
Public accounting firms, *see* Auditors
Public liability laws, 223
Public policy committee, 6

Quality Stores case, 35–39
Quarterly reports, 147
Quinn, John H. Jr., 33 n

Ratios, 175–177
Relationship, CEO and outside board
 members, 49
Reports, key ratios, 175–177
Resignation, 96
Retirement, *see* Board retirement policy
Rubber stamps, 53
Rushforth Company case, 106–110

Sage Company case, 99–106
San Francisco ballet, 202
Sayre International Center case, 214–219
Scott Company case, 134–137
Securities Act of 1933, 139–140

Securities and Exchange Commission:
  change in auditors, 151–152
  definition of directors' responsibilities,
    139–141, 143–144
  Foreign Corrupt Practices Act, 149
  Form 8-K, 143–144
  Form 10-Q, 147
Shapiro, Irving, 34
Smoothing earnings, 142–143
South Africa, 25
SRI International, 194
Staff assistance, to audit committee,
    150–151
Standards, 14, 24, 161–166, 221–222
Star and Moon case, 186–190
Stauder, Lloyd, 140
Stirling Homex case, 140, 144
Stock split, 183
Strategy:
  board's role, 4, 25–27, 223–224
  strategy meetings, 26–27
Succession for CEO:
  board responsibility, 3
  Japanese corporations, 232–235
  plans for, 23–24, 35–39, 88
  problems, 48–49, 60, 74–77, 83–86
Sunshine laws, 199
Support of CEO, 58

Takeovers:
  board responsibilities, 68–69
  crises situations, 63, 68–73
  defensive tactics, 70
  preparing for, 73
Tanner Corporation case, 153–158
Telemix Company case, 77–86
Townsend, Robert, 1
Trans Union Corporation, 141
Travel and entertainment expenses, audit
    of, 148
Tuchman, Barbara, 86
TWA, 70

Unfavorable developments, reporting,
    143–144
Union Carbide, 70
United Technologies, 64

Votes, 7, 12, 50

Warnaco, Inc., 140
Wendel, Bill, 23
Wyatt Company, 140

Young, John, 55

Zuckert, Eugene M., 2, 33 n